SWEET
and
DELICIOUS

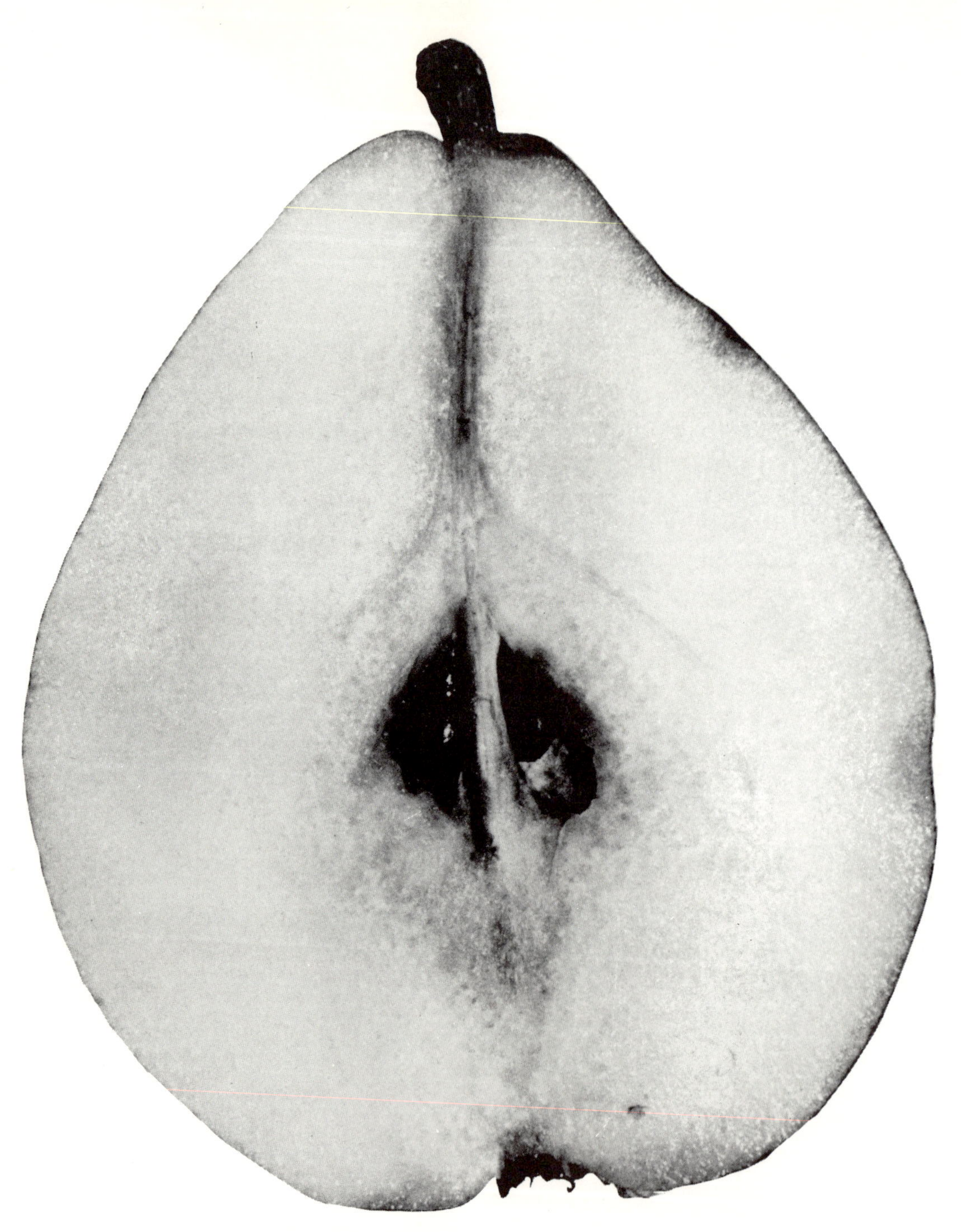

SWEET and DELICIOUS

Fruits of Tree, Bush and Vine

by Elizabeth K. Cooper and Padraic Cooper

photographs by Padraic Cooper

A GOLDEN GATE JUNIOR BOOK

Childrens Press, Chicago

Library of Congress Cataloging in Publication Data

Cooper, Elizabeth K.
    Sweet and delicious.

    SUMMARY: Traces the history and cultivation of such
fruits as the apple, banana, strawberry, and avocado.
Includes a variety of recipes.
    "A Golden Gate junior book."
    1. Fruit—Juvenile literature. 2. Fruit—culture—
Juvenile literature. 3. Cookery (Fruit) — Juvenile
literature. [1. Fruit. 2. Fruit culture. 3. Cookery — Fruit]
I. Cooper, Padraic, joint author.
II. Title.
SB355.C72   641.3′4   73-9713
ISBN 0-516-08742-8

ACKNOWLEDGEMENTS

The authors are indebted to the following organizations and individuals for their assistance in providing information and for facilitating laboratory and field research:

Sunkist Growers, Los Angeles, California

Calavo, Tropical Fruits, Los Angeles, California

Chiquita Brands, Inc., Boston, Massachusetts

The Dole Company, a Division of Castle & Cooke, Inc., Honolulu, Hawaii; and especially Dr. Steven J. Taussig, Director, Laboratories Service, and Mrs. Joann Rezents, Trade Relations Coordinator

Pineapple Research Institute, Wahiawa, Hawaii

Shields Date Gardens, Indio, California

CONTENTS

FRUIT
MARKET
PRODUCE

1

FRUITS of the EARTH

For a hike, a picnic, or a school lunch, there is nothing so handy as fruit. Fruit gives you drink when you are thirsty and quick energy when you are hungry. A good fruit is better than a sandwich. A sandwich must be made up and wrapped ahead of time, but an orange, banana, apple, or plum is always ready to go. Each is neatly packaged by nature, and just the right size to fit a hand or a pocket. Best of all, it is sweet, delicious—and good for you!

Many thousands of years ago, longer ago than most of us can imagine, people were hunters and gatherers. Families and tribes traveled from place to place, following wild animals and gathering food from the wild plants they found along the way. From the very beginning, people must have prized fruits for their convenience as well as for their taste and their value as food.

Today, we can only guess about the feelings of early man. There were no written records to tell us what life was really like in prehistoric times. But from gnawed bones, seeds, broken bits of pottery, and charred foods found among the rubbish and ashes of age-old fires, modern scientists have evidence that men of the Stone Age were plant eaters as well as meat eaters. They ate roots, stems, leaves, and especially seeds and fruits of wild plants.

Unlike roots and most other plant parts which early peoples used as food, fruits could be eaten easily. They did not have to be ground up, pounded, roasted, or boiled. They were good when eaten raw. This was important for people who seldom stayed long in any one place and had few if any pots or other cooking utensils.

After fruits had been picked or gathered, those not eaten at once could be put aside for later, and carried along when the family or tribe moved from one place to another. But fresh fruits, as you know, cannot be carried for too long. They soon become squishy and rotten and unfit for eating. However, in very early times, even without using pots, pans, or fire, people found a way to make their fruits last longer. They dried the wild fruits in the sun on hot summer days. The sun-dried fruits could then be stored for future use and could be carried along when the wandering people moved on. It was not hard to carry the dried fruits in folded leaves, straw baskets, clay jars, or in buckets made from tree bark or animal skin.

When you can, compare some dried fruits with some fresh ones of the same kinds. You will find that the dried ones are less juicy, but sweeter and chewier than the fresh ones. This is because most of the fresh fruits' water evaporates in the drying process. Also, sun drying usually increases the sugar content of the fruit. Each fruit weighs less when it is dried, and its food value is more concentrated.

As early man wandered, gathering fruits and carrying them from place to place, he ate the fruits and scattered the seeds. The eating of the fruits was important only to those who ate them. But the scattering of the seeds was important to future generations of people, from that time to this. For thousands of years, the travels of mankind have been ever westward, from the Far East of Asia to the Far West of the United States and Canada. So too have been the travels of most of the fruits we know best.

You know that apples and oranges are fruits. You can probably name many other fruits as well. But do you know *exactly* what a fruit is? Can you tell which of these are fruits?

strawberries	apples	dates
cucumbers	pears	grapefruits
grapes	green peas	tomatoes

If you say that they are all fruits, you are right. If you say that all but cucumbers, green peas, and tomatoes are fruits, you are also right! This is because the term *fruit* has more than one meaning. It has a scientific meaning and also a common, or popular, meaning.

A botanist is a scientist who studies plants. To a botanist, the seed-holding parts are the fruits of the plants on which they grow. This means that milkweed pods, chestnut burrs, pine cones, and the fuzzy white heads of dandelions—as well as plums, cherries, and grapes—are all fruits. But when you go to the supermarket for fruit for lunch, you will not find pine cones and weed pods in the fresh fruit section, nor canned dandelion heads among the canned fruits on the shelves.

When we think of fruits to eat, we usually think of things that are sweet, juicy, and delicious. The word *fruit* is from an old Latin word, "fructus," for enjoyment. A fruit is something to be enjoyed!

Of course we enjoy the "vegetable fruits" too, and our bodies need them for good nutrition. Most of the fruits we eat as vegetables are crops that must be planted each year. A cucumber vine or a green pea plant, for instance, comes up from a seed. It grows, flowers, bears fruits, and then dies, all in a single season. So do tomato, squash, pumpkin, and others. But a "fruit fruit"—one that we eat *as* a fruit— usually grows on a tree, vine, or other plant that lives, grows, and bears fruits year after year. Some apple trees have borne fruit for more than a hundred years. Wild fruits, as well as those cultivated by man, grow on plants that may live and bear for a very long time.

12

Fruits of the Earth

Our sweet, delicious, and beautifully colored fruits serve more than one purpose for the plants on which they grow. They not only hold the seeds and protect them as they develop, but also help spread the seeds when they are ripe. The sweet, juicy pulp attracts birds, other animals, and people. A fruit is ripe when its seed or seeds are ripe. Then the fruit has its special color—a shade of red, orange, yellow, green, blue, or purple. It is possible that the color as well as the scent of ripe fruit attracts animals from afar.

Birds are especially fond of berries and cherries. When they are ripe, flocks of birds pick them and fly off, eating and digesting the pulp and dropping the hard seeds. Since prehistoric times, berries and cherries have been among earth's most widely distributed plants.

Before the first explorers or settlers arrived on the North American continent from Europe, Indian people gathered wild fruits. But in those days there were only a few of the many kinds that grow here today. Cranberries, sharp and sour, grew wild in marshes along the northeast coast. Wild grapes hung in purple clusters from tangled vines in many areas. Berries of various kinds grew on thorny brambles in woodlands and on the plains. Wild strawberries, small but red and sweet, carpeted the ground in sunny open places. There were some fruit trees too—wild cherry, wild plum, and trees that bore hard little fruits like small crabapples.

North American Indians had none of the large, juicy

apples we have today. Indian children had no peaches, pears, apricots, oranges, lemons, grapefruit, bananas, figs, dates, melons or pineapples. All of these fruits had been growing for thousands of years in other lands, but none grew naturally where the United States and Canada are today.

Now in our markets we see many, many kinds of fruits, most of them grown in our own country. We see fresh fruits in bins, boxes, baskets, and bags. We see dried fruits on shelves. We see a great variety of canned fruits, jams, jellies, and fruit juices. Most of these delicious fruit treats that are now so abundant here had their beginnings in faraway lands. Each kind arrived here in its own time, in its own way, and has its own special story. Each kind gradually spread across America.

14

What kinds of fruits are sold in the markets in your neighborhood? When you eat a fresh fruit, examine its color, its scent, its sweet pulp, and its seed or seeds. You may want to start a collection of fruit seeds from raw or canned fruits. Or you may enjoy planting seeds from raw fruits and watching them grow.

As you investigate the fruits you eat, you can learn a bit about botany, the science of plants. You can find out about the work of travelers, settlers, explorers, planters, and scientists. And you can discover how, for thousands of years, people have been eating, planting, spreading, improving, and taking care of the fruits of the earth.

2

APPLES and other CORE FRUITS

"AS AMERICAN AS apple pie" is a common saying. "As American as cranberry sauce" would be much more accurate. Cranberries are true native fruits, which apples are not. Trees that bore edible apples did not grow here until they were brought across the ocean and planted by early settlers from Europe. English settlers planted apples in Virginia and New England, Dutch settlers planted them in New York, and settlers from France started apple trees in Canada.

At that time, apples were the most common fruit crop in central and northern Europe. But long, long before, they had been growing in southwest Asia, where they probably began in prehistoric times. Gradually, they spread westward across Europe, all before the beginning of written history.

In central Europe remains of the homes of Stone Age people show that fresh apples were eaten and stored, and apples were also cut up and dried in the sun.

In Norway, when a Viking ship was excavated not many

16

years ago, a bucket of apples was found on board. The apples are now wrinkled and brown, but they still look like apples. They were picked and packed in the wooden bucket over a thousand years ago!

Of course the apples from the ancient Viking ship are no longer edible. However, compared with other fruits, apples are unusually hardy. They keep well when they are properly stored in a cool place. Most of the fresh apples we eat in winter, spring, and early summer have been stored since picking time the autumn before.

Early settlers in America prized the apples for their hardiness as well as for their flavor, which is delicious both raw and cooked. They also prized them for cider, which was one of the main products of the many "apple plantations" of early America.

Apple trees grew well in the New World, and the settlers were soon sharing seeds and cuttings with the Indians. Some tribes planted apple orchards around their villages, and as their trees grew, they shared with other Indian tribes farther west. And so apple trees began to spread slowly across the land.

The westward spread of apples was helped by a most unusual man. His name was John Chapman, but everyone called him Johnny Appleseed. He believed in the Bible and in the goodness of people, animals, and apple trees. He was a wandering missionary, who traveled from one settlement to another in the frontier wilderness. On his head he wore a cooking pot in which he cooked his meals. On his back he bore a pack, for he liked to sleep outdoors under the trees. In his hands he carried his Bible and a bag of apple seeds, which he planted as he traveled from place to place.

Johnny Appleseed traveled for years, helping pioneer families plant apple trees around their cabins. He made friends with the Indians and with the wild animals of the forest, and he planted apple trees where otherwise none would have grown for years to come.

The spread of apple trees in our country seems to have kept up with the westward movement of settlers. After gold had been discovered in California, hordes of people crossed the continent in covered wagons. Others traveled by ship, some going all the way around the southern tip of South America. Many of these pioneers were prepared only to dig for gold. But some planned ahead for homes and apple trees. They brought with them switches cut from the branch tips of favorite trees. The cuttings were stuck in potatoes to keep them alive during the long months of travel. They carried apple seeds too, for these were easier to care for.

Most of America's best known apples came originally from seedling trees. However, planting seeds is not the most reliable way of getting good trees.

If we plant bean seeds from a good bean plant, the new plants are usually just like the plant that produced the seeds. But with apple and other fruit trees most of the

18

seedlings are not true to seed—not like the parent plant. Some may be poor trees that have inferior fruit. But among the average and the poor trees, there is always the chance of finding one unusually superior tree with fruits finer than any known at the time. Finding such a tree on one's own land is like discovering great treasure in one's own back yard.

In 1796 John McIntosh was clearing forest land not far from his home in Canada when he came upon a clump of about twenty young apple trees. Apples were a luxury where Mr. McIntosh lived, and so he carefully dug up the young trees and replanted them around his house.

For a while the trees grew well, but by 1830 all but one were dead. That one had grown rapidly, and each year it bore many red apples which were especially handsome and delicious. The owner and discoverer of the tree named it McIntosh Red. The tree continued to flourish, but in 1893 the McIntosh house caught fire and the apple tree was badly burned. However, one side of the tree lived on and continued to bear its wonderful apples until 1908. When it finally died, the original McIntosh Red had been bearing fruit for 112 years!

Through the years, many friends and neighbors were given cuttings from the old tree. Cuttings from this one great tree were the ancestors of all the trees that produce the abundance of McIntosh apples we see in our markets today.

A granite monument stands in Ontario, Canada bearing these words:

The original McIntosh Red Apple Tree stood about 20 rods north of this spot. It was one of a number of seedlings taken from the border of the clearings and transplanted by John McIntosh in the year 1796.

The first Baldwin apple tree was discovered in Wilmington, Massachusetts. The spot is marked by a tall stone pillar topped with a big stone apple. The tree that bore the first of the very popular Delicious apples was found in an orchard in Winterset, Iowa. But today our great apple growing areas are not in Ontario, Massachusetts, or Iowa, but in Washington and other northwestern states. However, there is no state in continental United States that does not grow apples.

An apple orchard is a ghostly place in the winter, for all the branches are bare, or white with mounds of snow. But in spring the leaf buds swell and fresh green leaves unfurl. Then come the flower buds in clusters, which open into delicate pink and white blossoms.

If you take an apple blossom apart you can see its seed-making parts. First, pull off the pink and white petals. Feel the pollen on the tips of the stamens. Pull off the stamens and examine the pistil through a magnifying glass. The moist stigma at the top of the pistil can hold onto any pollen grains that reach it. Split open the bottom of the pistil where there are little ovules, which will develop into

seeds. But before ovules can become seeds, the flower must be pollinated and the ovules must be fertilized.

Bees visit the fragrant flowers to sip nectar, a sweet, watery liquid which they use in making honey. As a bee dips into an apple blossom, pollen from the stamens collects on its velvety coat and in pollen baskets on its legs. Some of the pollen then falls off the bee when it brushes against sticky stigmas in other blossoms.

Material from grains of pollen then fertilize the ovules in the ovary at the bottom of each blossom. Only when they are fertilized can the ovules develop into seeds and the fruits form and ripen. So, for the apples we eat, we depend not only on the people who grow them, but also on the feeding activities of little bees.

When you eat an apple or pear, you probably throw away the core. The core is a strong, papery chamber that encloses the part of the fruit that holds the seeds. Core fruits are called pomes. Apples, pears, and quinces are pome fruits. The quince, a hard, round yellow fruit, is not eaten raw. It is seldom seen or used today, except for making jelly. Pears, however, are very plentiful and popular.

Examine a whole apple or pear. Observe the stem end, where it was attached to the tree. Notice the blossom end. You can see some of the flower parts that were left after the petals fell off. If you cut a pome fruit in half from stem end to blossom end, you can get one view of the form of the core. Then, if you cut another one in half the other

way, you can see good cross-sections of the papery chamber and the seeds.

Pears, like apples, have been enjoyed since prehistoric times. They were eaten by people of the Stone Age, and were popular in ancient Egypt, Greece, Syria, Rome, and other ancient lands. Before Columbus set off on his voyages of discovery, many kinds of pears were being grown in Europe.

Early settlers brought pear seeds and young pear trees to these shores. By 1770 one nursery near New York was selling more than forty different kinds of pear trees. Some bore juicy, delicious fruits called butter pears because of the melting softness of their flesh. They were similar to the Bartlet pears of today.

For a few years all went well in the pear orchards. Then a disease known as "fire blight" swept through the eastern orchards, killing pear trees, especially the popular butter pears. The blight was caused by bacteria that attacked roots

23

and bark and made leaves wither as though they had been burned. The blight was uncontrollable in eastern orchards for many years, and so the growing of choice butter pears moved westward, to areas where the summers were relatively dry. (In fairly recent years, modern "wonder drugs" have been used sucessfully against the bacteria that cause fire blight.)

Meanwhile, sand pears from China and Japan were being grown in eastern gardens for the beauty of their early spring blossoms. These trees could withstand the blight, but their fruits were hard and gritty. They were sometimes used in making preserves, but they could not be eaten raw.

One day, Peter Kieffer, a gardener in Philadelphia, noticed the leaves on one of the young sand pear trees. They were like those on some soft-fruited Bartlet pears that grew nearby. The young tree was a hybrid, a cross between a sand pear and a Bartlet pear. It must have grown from a seed from a sand pear blossom that had been pollinated by pollen from a Bartlet blossom.

Mr. Kieffer was interested in the hybrid tree. He carefully transplanted it and took care of it until it matured and bore fruits. This was a hundred years ago, and the fruits were the first Kieffer pears, which are still grown today. The trees are resistant to blight, and the fruits are softer and less gritty than the original sand pears. In time, various kinds of blight-resistant trees were developed from the hardy sand pears of Asia.

24

In California, Oregon, and Washington, the finest of the soft European butter pears are grown. Different people prefer different kinds of pears. And so, in our markets today we find pears of many different kinds. Some are so soft and juicy that they are eaten with a spoon, and others are so hard and sandy that one bite sets one's teeth on edge. Between these extremes, we have a wide variety in flavor, texture, size, and color. We are indeed a pear-rich land!

If you like pears, you may like to make this special pear dessert. It is easy to make and needs no cooking.

HONEY PEAR DESSERT

You will need one large, soft, fully ripe pear for every two people.

Cut each pear in half from stem end to blossom end. Put each half on a saucer. Cut out the cores and fill the holes with honey. If you have no honey, sprinkle the cut side of each pear with brown sugar.

Chill the pears in the refrigerator. For dessert, eat the sweetened pear flesh with a spoon, getting a bit of honey or brown sugar with each small spoonful of pear.

3

ORANGES
the GOLDEN
CITRUS BERRIES

CITRUS IS THE name the ancient Romans gave to the citron tree. The fruit looks like a large lemon with rough, bumpy skin. It has a small amount of sour pulp and is used mainly for its thick peel, which is candied and put into fruit cakes and plum puddings. One species of citron, the Etrog, or sacred Jewish citron, is used by Jews at the Feast of Tabernacles. The small, greenish-yellow fruit is carried in a religious ceremony of thanksgiving.

Some scientists think that the citron may be the world's oldest kind of citrus plant. Whether it is or not, its ancient Roman name has been given to the important plant family which includes oranges, grapefruit, lemons, limes, and other juicy, delicious fruits.

To botanists, the fruits of citrus trees are berries. Like

26

other true berries, their seeds have no hard, stony coverings and are in pulpy flesh that is enclosed in a skin or rind.

Cut an orange in half and observe its cross section. The structure is typical of berries that grow on citrus trees. In the middle is a soft central axis. Radiating from it are segments of juicy pulp. Notice how the seeds, usually near the axis, are embedded in the pulp. Feel the inner part of the rind, which is soft and spongy. Smell the outer part of the rind, which has many tiny oil glands. If you hold a piece of fresh peel near your face and squeeze it, you will feel and smell a spray of fragrant oil.

Among the many citrus fruits, oranges are the best known and most important. They probably began in Asia. Perhaps they were natives of southern China and Indochina, where wild orange trees can still be found. Of course, we cannot know for sure just where the first ones grew because orange trees have been living on the earth since prehistoric times.

The fruits of wild orange trees of the past were bright, seedy little berries with a sharp, spicy scent and a sour, bitter taste. From them was once made a bitter drink that was used as medicine.

The ancient Chinese were probably the first people in the world to cultivate oranges. More than four thousand years ago, Chinese scholars mentioned oranges in some of their writings. Cared for by skilled fruit growers, who knew how to save and plant the seeds from only the biggest and best fruits, the small golden berries became less sour and less seedy through the years—and more desirable as fruits. Nevertheless, the spread of oranges to other lands was a very slow process.

Year after year for centuries, orange seeds were carried westward by birds and other small animals. In time, seeds, cuttings, and young trees were also carried westward by men. Arab traders, who traveled widely through many regions of the world, were especially fond of the orange tree. They prized it not only for its fruits, but also for its fragrant waxy white blossoms and deep green leaves that stayed on the tree all through the year.

As Arab people moved from land to land and from one continent to another, they planted groves of orange trees. In time, the golden fruits were being grown in most of the warm areas of Africa and Europe as well as in Asia where they had begun. Oranges grew especially well in Spain, the homeland of early explorers of Florida. It is said that Ponce de León and his men planted orange seeds when they first came to Florida. Later, in 1565, when the city of St. Augustine was settled, the Spanish settlers brought seeds and cuttings from the orange groves of Spain.

Florida Indians, who enjoyed the tart, refreshing fruits, would carry them to their villages, which were usually on the banks of lakes or streams. The Indians ate the fruits and scattered the seeds on the ground which was just right for growing orange trees. The seeds sprouted and grew into trees and, in time, the trees bore fruits. The fruits had seeds, which grew into more orange trees. And so the oranges multiplied and kept on multiplying. Two hundred years later, when other settlers came to Florida, they found groves of Spanish orange trees growing wild. One grove was forty miles long! Untended, the trees had spread in areas where the Indians had once had their villages.

Early explorers and settlers from Portugal, where oranges grew as well as they did in Spain, planted the first orange trees in South America. In Brazil the trees did so well and spread so fast that later settlers thought that oranges were native Brazilian trees. But, like the Florida orange groves, the first had been started with seeds and cuttings that had survived a long, slow voyage in a sailing ship across the Atlantic Ocean.

Spanish missionary priests, or padres, came to Mexico to convert the Indians to Christianity. They taught the Indians Spanish customs and the Spanish language and worked to spread the religion of Spain in the New World. Wherever the padres settled, they built missions for worship and teaching and planted fruit orchards from seeds and cuttings brought over from Spain. Oranges were among the imported fruit trees that grew beautifully in Mexico, as they still do today.

In 1769, some of the padres moved northward into California, where again they built missions. They named the missions for favorite saints—San Diego, San Gabriel, Santa Barbara, Santa Clara, San Francisco—names that California

30

cities bear today. As soon as a new mission was begun, the padres and their Indian helpers planted orange trees from seeds and cuttings from the orchards in Mexico. A planting of four hundred trees at Mission San Gabriel was California's first citrus orchard of any size.

Today, our two leading orange-growing states are California and Florida. In both states the first orange trees were planted by Spaniards.

Throughout the long history of oranges, there have been three main kinds, each with many varieties. The most important kind, especially in the western world, is the sweet orange. It is juicy, fairly sweet, and has a tightly fitting skin.

A second kind is the mandarin orange, which has a thin, loose skin that is easily removed. In China and Japan, mandarin oranges are preferred. The tangerine is a kind of mandarin orange. It developed from mandarins in North Africa, and was named for the North African port of Tangiers. From there the Arabs brought the fruits into Spain. The tangerine is sometimes called the "kid-glove orange" because its skin can be pulled off so easily. Once the skin is off, the segments practically separate by themselves.

A third main kind of orange is the sour, bitter Seville orange. It is tart and too sour to be enjoyed when eaten raw. However, oranges of this kind are delicious when made into marmalade, for which they are commonly used, especially in England and Scotland, where the Seville oranges are shipped in from Spain. If you read the labels on jars of marmalade in a big supermarket, you will find some with words like these: *Made from genuine Seville oranges,* or, *Nothing but sugar and Seville bitter oranges.* Such marmalade has more tang and a sharper, richer taste than that made from the sweet oranges grown in the United States.

Through thousands of years, as the golden citrus berry gradually moved westward, it has had different names in different languages. Yet, as you see from the list below, some of the names are alike, or seem to be closely related.

NAGRUNGA . . . . Ancient Sanskrit
NARANJ . . . . Arab
NARANJA . . . . Spanish
ARANCIA . . . . Italian
LARANJA . . . . Portuguese
ORANGE . . . . French, English, German

Orange trees cannot grow in countries like Canada, Germany, or England. Nor can they grow in most parts of the United States. Like other citrus trees, they need a warm, but not hot, climate. Too much heat, as well as not enough, can damage the fruits and even kill the trees. So, for many generations, the orange was a rare and expensive fruit in many parts of the world.

In our own country it was a treat for children in northern states to receive an orange as a gift or find one in the toe of a Christmas stocking. Today, with fast trucks, trains, and ships, and ever-faster planes, fresh oranges are in food mar-

kets all over the world. Though oranges are no longer rare or expensive, they are still most precious. They are not only sweet, juicy, and delicious, but also rich in vitamin C, which the human body needs daily for good health.

California's orange-growing industry began seven years before the Gold Rush of 1849. It was started by William Wolfskill, who had spent most of his days as a hunter and trapper in the West. Tired of the cold and hardships of the mountains and wilderness, he came to a warm, sunny land where the streets and buildings of downtown Los Angeles are today. There, in the dusty little pueblo of Los Angeles, he planted young orange and lemon trees, which he had obtained from the San Gabriel Mission gardens a few miles away.

The trees grew well, and in time Mr. Wolfskill had seventy acres of orange and lemon trees. Then, when the little pueblo of Los Angeles was linked by transcontinental railroad to the rest of the country, Mr. Wolfskill filled freight cars with freshly picked fruit and shipped it east to St. Louis. This was in 1877, and the fruit was a whole month on the way. Nevertheless, most of it was in good condition when it arrived, and it was eagerly bought by fruit-hungry people.

Through the years, as more and more oranges were grown in California and in Florida, the fruits were getting better—more juicy, less sour, fewer seeds. One of the most startling improvements was made, not by climate, soil, or by the skill of the growers, but by nature. It happened about a hundred and fifty years ago in Brazil. A worker was busy in an orange orchard when he noticed some large fruits that looked strangely deformed. Each had a bumpy growth on the blossom end. The worker picked one of the fruits, cut it open, and tasted it. It was sweet. It was juicy. And it had no seeds!

The worker examined the fruits on trees growing nearby. Only one branch of that one tree had the big, funny-looking fruits. They were true freaks of nature—natural variations of normal oranges. Each was really a double orange, with a small fruit growing out of a larger one. You can see this when you examine one of the big seedless fruits we now call navel oranges. The "navel" is where the smaller orange is growing out from the larger one.

The Brazilian worker cut buds from the branch that bore the new fruits. For each bud, he made a T-shaped cut in the bark of a young orange tree. He worked the bud into the cut, fitted it under the bark, and then tied up the cut. The buds grew into strong branches. In time, they bore the big, seedless double oranges.

Fifty years went by, and then, about a hundred years

ago, a woman traveler from the United States saw the navel oranges growing in Brazil. She and her husband sent some budded cuttings to the Department of Agriculture in Washington, D.C. The first shipment arrived dry and lifeless, but a second shipment, in 1870, contained twelve newly budded trees in good condition. Most of them died later, but three of them were sent to Mr. and Mrs. Tibbetts, of Riverside, California. They planted the young budded trees not far from the back door of their farmhouse. A wandering cow destroyed one of the trees, but the others survived. When rain was scarce, Mrs. Tibbetts watered them with the dishwater every time she did the dishes. The trees thrived on the Tibbetts' farm, and in 1875 they bore their first fruits. They were big, sweet, juicy, and seedless—the first of the now famous California navel oranges.

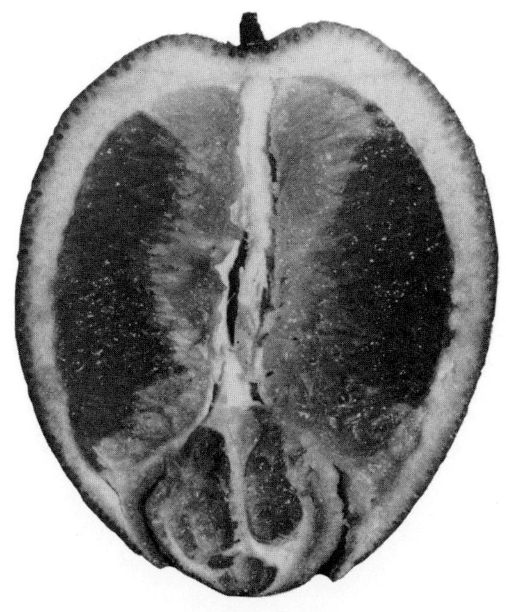

As more and more settlers arrived in the Riverside area, many came to the Tibbetts' farm for "budstock"—buds they could graft onto seedling trees of their own. People were glad to pay the price the Tibbetts asked—five dollars a bud, which in those days was more than many people earned in a week. Even so, the buyers got a bargain, for the climate and soil of California were ideal for the new kind of orange.

Today, navel oranges grown in the California-Arizona area are harvested from November through May and shipped to all parts of our country and to many foreign countries as well. Another variety of sweet orange, the Valencia, grows in the same areas. Valencia oranges are lighter in color than navels, have some seeds, and have sweet, juicy pulp. They are harvested from February to November. Thus, with navel oranges in late fall and winter, and Valencias the rest of the time, California has oranges ripening all through the year.

If you like the taste of fresh oranges, as most people do, here is a dessert to make for yourself and your friends. It is good enough to serve to company, even as part of a special holiday meal.

ICY CITRUS SURPRISE

To serve four, you will need two oranges and a pint of orange, lemon, or grapefruit ice or sherbet.

Cut the oranges in half and squeeze out the juice. Try to leave a little of the juicy pulp on the inside of each of the orange shells. Put the juice away to drink later. Then spoon the ice or sherbet into each of the shells, packing it down and smoothing it into a mound on the top. If you have any citrus trees in your yard, pick a few very small leaves, wash them well, and stick one or two into the top of each icy mound. Put each dessert into a sandwich bag and keep it in the refrigerator freezer until serving time.

A similar dessert can be made in shells from small, squeezed-out grapefruits.

4

LEMONS, LIMES and GRAPEFRUIT

When Columbus sailed the seas, and for many years before and many years after his time, ocean voyages were long and dangerous. Ships' crews were in peril not only from the seas beneath them and the storms above, but also from the food and drink on board. Supplies of fresh water often ran low and became undrinkable. For long periods of time, the only foods were hard, dry, and often spoiled. On some voyages, the sailors lived for weeks at a time on salt beef and hardtack—thick, rock-hard crackers.

Men on the early sailing ships suffered from scurvy, and many died of it. On one of his voyages, Vasco da Gama, the Portuguese navigator, lost a hundred out of a hundred and sixty men to the fearsome disease. But, for hundreds of years, no one knew the cause of scurvy. In time, however, it was observed that men who ate citrus fruits or drank the juice did not get scurvy, and so lemons and limes were carried on ships and fed to the crews. This is how British seamen gained the nickname, "Limeys."

On long voyages, sailors took their rations of citrus for many years before scientists discovered the cause of scurvy and why citrus fruits prevent it. Scurvy is a deficiency disease caused by lack of vitamin C in the diet. It affects teeth, bones, blood, and general health. Lemons, limes, oranges, and other citrus fruits are rich in vitamin C, supplying enough of this essential vitamin to prevent scurvy, even though the rest of the diet may be poor, as it usually was on the sailing ships of the past.

Today, with refrigeration and all kinds of canned and frozen foods, we are not likely to suffer from scurvy. Nevertheless, we all need vitamin C each day, and a pleasant way to get it is by drinking a glass of juice from a citrus fruit.

Lemons and limes are the "ade fruits." In most parts of the world, lemonade and limeade are favorite drinks. These two fruits are also widely used to add tang and flavor to salads, meats, desserts, and other foods. Like the orange, these two closely related fruits began somewhere in the Far East and were carried westward to other warm lands by the Arabs.

Between the years 1000 and 1200 A.D., Crusaders returning to their homes in Europe told of the wonderful fruit trees that grew in Arab lands. Some brought home lemon seeds from Palestine and planted them around their castles in southern Italy and Spain.

The first lemons and limes in North and South America were brought over by Spanish explorers and settlers. Limes, it was found, grew best in tropical and semi-tropical areas. Lemons, which also needed warmth, did not thrive in the high humidity of the tropics. They needed a more moderate climate, neither too cold in winter nor too hot in summer. Today, most of the limes in our markets are from southern Florida and Mexico. Most of the lemons are from the mild coastal regions of California.

When you drive or walk through a lemon-growing area, you are surrounded by waves of fragrance. Lemon trees have sweet-scented blossoms, tiny green fruits, and ripe yellow fruits all year long. How different from apple and

most other fruit trees! These lose their leaves in winter, and then pass from buds to flowers to fruits, one stage at a time. But, if you look closely at a lemon tree, you may find blossoms and fruits in different stages on a single branch.

If you like the sharp, sour-sweet taste of lemons, you can make a special treat for yourself.

Lemon-on-a-Stick

Get a large fresh lemon and a stick of peppermint candy. Make a hole in one end of the lemon, and squeeze until you see juice in the hole. Then work the bottom of the candy stick into the juicy hole. Suck on the top of the stick as though it were a drinking straw. Small amounts of tart lemon juice will be drawn up through tiny openings in the candy stick. The flavor of sweet peppermint mixed with lemon is delicious.

Lemon-on-a-Stick is a very old American treat that children used to have on holidays, especially on the Fourth of July.

Limes as well as lemons are yellow when they are fully ripe. In our country sour, green limes are preferred, and those we see in markets have been picked when fully grown but not yet yellow-ripe. There are sweet limes as well as sweet lemons, and the sweet ones are preferred in some eastern lands. We, however, like our limes and our lemons sharp and sour.

Oranges, lemons, and limes were being used all over the rest of the world long before the Americas were dreamed of. But the grapefruit became famous only after it was commonly used as a breakfast fruit in the United States. In a way, the grapefruit belongs to the New World, though its ancestor, the pummelo, probably originated in far-away Southeast Asia. The pummelo is a huge, slightly soft yellow fruit as big as a man's head. Its skin is thick, and its pulp is rather tasteless, with none of the sharp, fruity tang of grapefruit. For years, pummelo trees were grown in gardens as interesting curiosities. The gigantic fruits were once called "Adam's apples."

Late in the 1600's, Captain Shaddock, commander of one of the East Indian ships, stopped in the West Indies on one of his long voyages. He left some pummelo seeds on the island of Barbados. The seeds were planted. They sprouted and grew into large trees, which bore their large yellow fruits. In time, the pummelos became known as shaddocks. The shaddocks flourished on Barbados and spread to other islands of the West Indies.

No one knows exactly when or how the first grapefruit tree grew from a shaddock, or pummelo, seed. It probably happened naturally, as a mutation. That is, one shaddock seedling was different from the others, and different from the parent tree on which it grew. The differences were not just for that one seedling tree, but would be inherited by its offspring, and by their offspring. The mutant—the tree that was different—had fruits that were not huge and coarse like those that grew on the shaddock trees. The new fruits were smaller, more fragrant, and had thinner, finer skin. At first they were called "forbidden fruits." Later, they became known as grapefruits, probably because they sometimes grew in clusters, like bunches of giant yellow grapes.

Early in the 1800's a Spanish nobleman brought seeds of the new fruit to Florida. At first, the trees were grown mainly as decorative garden plants. At the beginning of the 1900's, the grapefruit was still just a novelty fruit, unknown to most people. But, ten years later, Florida-grown grapefruit was being shipped regularly to northern states. It soon became a common and popular fruit throughout the United

States. Gradually, its popularity spread from there to other countries.

Today, grapefruit is grown in Florida, California, Arizona, and Texas, as well as in citrus-growing areas of other lands. In big markets, we now have our choice of big fruits, small ones, grapefruit with pink flesh and grapefruit with "white" (really, pale yellow) flesh. The early grapefruits were very seedy, but most of those grown today have few seeds. However, if you look carefully when you cut open a grapefruit, you can usually find some seeds to save for planting.

AN INDOOR GRAPEFRUIT GROVE

Fill an aluminum foil loaf pan with garden soil or planter mix. Water the soil and work it well to make it damp but not muddy. Plant grapefruit seeds about one-fourth-inch deep and an inch apart. Then cover the pan with a tent of transparent plastic wrap to make a little hothouse.

Keep the planter in a window or other light, warm spot. If there is not much sunlight where you live, put your little hothouse under a lighted lamp for a few hours each evening.

Watch the soil for signs of sprouting. It may take three or four weeks before the first green stems break through to the light. If the plastic wrap is fitted tightly around the pan, it should not be necessary to add water, for water from the soil will evaporate and then condense on the inside of the plastic, keeping the soil and seedlings moist.

When the plants are about one inch tall, take off the plastic. From then on, water gently whenever the soil looks and feels dry, daily if necessary.

When still only a few inches high, grapefruit seedlings look like tiny trees, each with a sturdy, trunk-like stem and shiny green leaves. They can then be transplanted to ordinary flower pots. With proper care, they will grow into handsome indoor plants that make welcome gifts.

Using the same procedures, plant seeds from oranges, lemons, or tangerines. These too can grow into plants that do well in the house, in the moderate temperature that is comfortable for you.

For hundreds of years, people have been growing citrus trees indoors. Wealthy people who lived in countries where the winters were too cold for citrus trees had orange and lemon trees planted in big tubs of soil. These were placed in rows in large, beautiful rooms they called "orangeries." The orangeries had many windows and were heated by stoves in the cold months of winter. Expert gardeners tended the trees, which had flowers and bore fruits in the indoor environment. In time, the orangeries were used for many kinds of flowering and foliage plants from warm lands. When the owners had parties their guests would stroll through the orangeries, admiring the plants, inhaling the fragrance of flowers in bloom, and perhaps eating a freshly picked citrus fruit as the snow came down outdoors.

5

THE PRUNUS FAMILY PLUMS, PEACHES, and other STONE FRUITS

DID YOU EVER take a good look at a dried prune? Its skin is black and puckered up in deep wrinkles. When you squeeze it, you can feel the hard pit inside. On one end you can see a tiny hole left by the stem from which the fruit hung as it grew and ripened on the tree.

Dried prunes are chewy and have a sweet, fruity taste. They are handy quick-energy snacks, better than candy or gum. After you have looked over a couple of prunes, eat them and save the pits.

Feel one of the pits and notice its hard, stony covering. You cannot crack it open with your fingers. To open some prune pits, put them inside a plastic sandwich bag. Lay the bag on something solid—a breadboard, brick, or flat stone. Using a hammer, hit the pits just hard enough to crack open the hard shells. Then empty the plastic bag and pick out the seeds. They look very much like small nuts.

The Prunus Family

If you take a little bite of one of the seeds you will discover that it also tastes like a nut.

Prune seeds taste like almonds. This is not surprising, for almonds and prunes are related. They belong to the Prunus family, which is a large plant family indeed. It includes all the fruits that have a single seed in a hard, stony pit, enclosed in a layer of pulp. Botanists call such fruits one-seed drupe fruits. A more common name for them is stone fruits. The drupes, or stone fruits, include plums, peaches, apricots, almonds, and cherries. All but the almonds are grown for their delicious juicy pulp. Almonds, whose pulp is woody and dry, are prized for their seeds. Hence, almonds are used as nuts, not fruits.

The family Prunus was named for the Latin word for plum. Prunes are cured dried plums. Plums have been on the earth for so long that their beginnings are lost in the misty shadows of the past. Fossils of plums have been found in rock layers that were formed six million years before the first people began to live on this planet.

In prehistoric times, one species of wild plum grew in Europe and another species in Asia. No one can be sure where the first ones grew or how plums spread to the continent of North America. The seeds may have been brought here by birds, or by primitive men who somehow reached here from Asia. In any case, we know that plums have been growing on this continent for a very long time. They are the most widely distributed native fruit trees in America.

47

Early settlers from Europe found wild plum trees from Florida to New England. Later, as pioneers traveled westward in covered wagons, they found plums from the east coast to the Rocky Mountains, and in several areas beyond the Rockies. The wild fruits were important to the early settlers and pioneers, whose diet was otherwise dull and monotonous. The plums they gathered in the wilderness of the new land were not as big, juicy, or sweet as those we buy in markets today. But they were delicious when stewed or made into jam, jelly, or plum butter. Even today, people gather plums from wild trees and bushes and make them into spreads for biscuits and bread.

If you live near a natural history museum, you may be able to find out there, from someone in the botany department, where wild plum trees grow in your area.

For many years, settlers in the east not only gathered wild plums but also raised plum trees from seeds and cuttings from their homelands in Europe. In most parts of the country, European plums are now the most important species. First in importance are the drying plums, known as prunes. These dark-colored plums are dried with their pits in, outdoors in the sun or indoors in huge dehydrators.

Another kind of European plum that is common here is the yellowish-green Riene Claude, which was named in France almost five hundred years ago for Queen Claudia. When Sir William Gage, an Englishmen, took some of the handsome fruits home to England, the plums were called

Greengages. Many varieties of Greengage plums are now grown in our country.

Luther Burbank, the great American plant breeder, became interested in Japanese plums. He imported many kinds and improved them by cross-breeding. This is done by using pollen from one variety of plum tree to pollinate the blossoms on a plum tree of another kind. The offspring of such cross-breeding are called hybrids. A hybrid inherits some characteristics from one parent and some from the other. Many hybrids are no better than either of the parent plants. Some are less good. But a few inherit the best traits of both parents. Such hybrids become superior trees that bear superior fruits.

Cross-breeding goes on all the time as wind, rain, and especially bees carry pollen from blossom to blossom. It is also done by scientists and growers as they work with nature to produce better and better fruits of all kinds.

The peach, another member of the Prunus family, is one of the world's most useful fruits. It can be eaten whole, like an apple. It can be sliced and served on breakfast cereal or by itself as a dessert. It can also be dried, cooked, canned, spiced, pickled, made into jam, frozen in ice cream, or baked in a pie. The word "peachy" was once commonly used to describe somebody or something super-wonderful. The peach is indeed a peachy fruit!

The peach got its name because of a mistake. The fruit was once called "Persian apple." The word "peach" is from the Latin word for Persian. For more than two thousand years, people thought that peaches had first grown in Persia. But, in modern times, botanists have found native peach trees in China, and have learned that peaches were written about in Chinese literature about four thousand years ago—long, long before they were known elsewhere. Though they originated in ancient China, it is too late now to change the fruit's name from "Persian" to "Chinese."

The peach traveled westward along the old trading routes as traders carried peach pits from China and traded them along the way. In time, peaches reached Greece and Rome, then spread through Europe. European settlers brought the peach to the New World. The Spanish introduced peaches into Mexico and later into California. The French brought them to Louisiana. English colonists planted peach trees in Virginia, and the Pilgrims planted them in New England.

American Indians, eager for new fruits, started peach orchards of their own. From one village to the next, peach trees spread from pits that were scattered or planted by Indians.

Most of the peach trees grown here today are superior descendants of the earlier trees. Generation after generation, as superior seedlings were selected and given special care, American-grown peaches improved. Through the years, plant breeders have worked with peaches, cross-breeding and developing new hybrids, seeking larger, meatier, more fragrant, and more flavorful fruits.

When ripe peaches are in season, notice the different kinds on display in a big food market. At any time of the year, notice the many kinds of canned peaches on the shelves. We are truly a peach-growing, peach-eating country.

When you eat a raw peach, you not only wash it first, but you probably rub off at least some of the fuzz. Peach fuzz may not be very tasty, but it seems to help protect the ripe fruit from injuries and insects. One kind of peach, however, has skin that is smooth and soft, with no fuzz at all. We call this fruit the nectarine, and it has been known in some lands for about two thousand years. Nectarines are real peaches and they grow on typical peach trees. Like other peaches, the fruits may be clingstone or freestone and may have pale yellow, golden, or reddish pulp. But the nectarines fine, fuzzless skins make them more delicate—harder to pick, pack, store, and ship. For this reason, nectarines are less commonly used in northern and eastern states than in California and other Far Western states where many of them are raised.

The apricot is another drupe fruit that belongs to the Prunus family. It looks like a small golden peach, but it is another kind of Prunus, with history and legends of its own. Like many of our favorite fruits, apricots first grew in China.

Long, long ago, according to an ancient Chinese tale, a child was born who was so wise that he could talk on the day of his birth. He was born outdoors, under a flowering apricot tree. As he looked up into its branches, the newborn baby chose his name. He called himself by the Chinese word for apricot. He lived long and taught the people of China a new religion. He became known as Lao-tse, which means "Old Master" in Chinese. But the childhood name of this brilliant boy may well have been "Apricot." Our English word for the fruit is from the Latin for "early maturing" or "ripening beforehand." These terms describe apricots, which ripen early, and might also describe a child who is able to talk on the day he is born.

From China, apricots spread westward to Europe in ancient times. They were grown in Greece and Rome. From there they spread to Spain and throughout Europe, all before the time of Columbus. The Spanish carried apricots to Mexico, and the English brought them to Virginia. Later, Spanish padres from Mexico brought apricots northward to California and planted them in mission gardens.

Unlike plums, apricots do not thrive in the northern and eastern areas of North America. The trees are not only early to ripen, but also early to flower. This means that the blossoms open so early in spring that they are often blighted by frost. Also, ripe apricots have soft pulp and delicate skin. They cannot survive hard rains or extreme heat without cracking and decaying.

Tough apricots, imported from Siberia and Manchuria, are now grown in northern areas, mainly for family eating and home canning. Most of the fresh and canned apricots we buy are raised west of the Rocky Mountains, especially in California. There, tons and tons of ripe apricots are grown each year for shipping, canning, and drying.

Apricots for market sales and for canning must be carefully picked by hand. But the ones to be dried can be left until they are fully ripe and then shaken from the trees. The fruits are then cut in half and the pits are removed. The halves are spread in shallow trays and exposed to fumes of burning sulfur for a half hour to two or three hours. This is done to preserve the fruit's bright golden color.

After the sulfuring, the apricots are dried outdoors in the

sun. In the drying process, water evaporates from the fruit and the sugar content increases. It takes about six pounds of fresh apricots to make one pound of dried ones. Thus, one little dried apricot half has about three times the food value of a whole fresh apricot.

Some people object to sulfur fumes or any other chemical substance added to food. They buy untreated dried apricots, which are brownish rather than golden in color. Look for different kinds of dried fruits and read the labels on the bags or boxes. Dried fruits are sold in ordinary markets and also in stores that specialize in health foods.

All trees that bear stone fruits are particularly beautiful in spring when their delicate branches are covered with clusters of pink, white, or pink-and-white flowers. The best known in our country are the Japanese flowering cherry trees in Washington, D.C. Thousands of people visit our capital city each year when the cherry trees are in bloom. These trees, like some species of plum, peach, and apricot, are not grown for their fruits but for beautiful blossoms.

In our country, we grow two main kinds of cherry trees for their fruits—the sweet, or bird cherry, and the sour, or pie cherry. Both kinds began in Asia and eastern Europe and spread westward in prehistoric times.

Sweet cherries were spread mainly by birds, which ate the luscious fruits and scattered the seeds with their droppings. Heaps of sweet cherry pits have been found in European cave dwellings. So we know that sweet cherries grew

in Europe in very early times and were gathered and eaten by Stone Age people. Sour cherries, however, traveled westward more slowly. The sour fruits were less appealing to birds, and so they arrived in Europe later, as westward-moving people scattered their seeds.

Cherry trees and their fruits were described by writers in ancient Greece and ancient Rome. In about 50 B.C., a Roman wrote a book about farming. In it he discussed cherries and told about grafting, a practice still used in fruit growing today, more than 2,000 years later.

In grafting, a shoot, bud, twig, or branch (called a cion) from a good tree is fitted into a cut made in the trunk of a sturdy, well-rooted seedling. If the graft "takes," the cion becomes the tree's main branch, from which other branches grow. The fruits borne on grafted trees are exactly like those produced by the trees from which the cions were cut. Superior trees can be reproduced more dependably by grafting than by planting their seeds. Fruits from grafts are exact reproductions, while fruits from seedlings may be less good than those on the parent tree.

As soon as the Dutch, French, and English colonists settled in America, they began to cultivate cherries from their homelands. We know that cherry trees were growing at Mt. Vernon in Virginia when George Washington was a little boy, though some people are not sure that he chopped one of them down with his little hatchet.

Most of the cherries grown in our country today are kinds

that were brought here from Europe. However, the Bing, our best-known sweet cherry, originated here. Like the McIntosh apple, it began as a chance seedling that was different. Its superior qualities were recognized, and the seedling was selected for cultivation and reproduction.

Sweet cherry trees are self-sterile. Pollen from one tree cannot pollinate the blossoms on the same tree, or on another tree of the same variety. For this reason, a sweet cherry orchard is planted with different varieties of sweet cherry trees. Bees do the pollinating, transferring pollen from a tree of one variety to one of another. If there are not enough bees in the area, an orchard grower may buy or even rent hives and place them near his cherry orchards at blossom time.

Sour cherries are self-pollinating. Pollen from one tree can pollinate the flowers on the same tree or on another tree of the same kind. Bees pollinate both sweet and sour cherry blossoms, and also the blossoms of other stone-fruit trees.

As you know, all stone fruits are sold fresh, to be eaten raw, just as they come from the trees. Each kind of stone fruit is available for only a short time each year, during the few weeks in summer or early fall at harvest time. Most of the year, we buy the fruits dried or canned or made into jam.

You can make a delicious stone-fruit sauce even in winter. You can make it from canned fruits.

SWEET STONE-FRUIT STEW

Use about a cupful (one 8-ounce can) of each of the following fruits: peaches, apricots, plums, and sweet cherries. Use fruits that have been canned in heavy syrup. Remove the pits and cut the fruits into small pieces.

Put the mixed fruits and syrupy juices into a cooking pot. Add one cupful of granulated sugar and stir well. Put the pot on the stove over medium-low heat and stir until the mixture begins to boil. Let it simmer gently for 30 minutes. Stir from time to time to prevent sticking.

Test for the right thickness by putting a spoonful onto a cool saucer. Stir it, and then taste it as soon as it cools. When the sauce is as thick as you want, take it off the stove. Let it cool, and then spoon it into clean glasses or jars. Cover each one with foil or plastic wrap. Store the sauce in the refrigerator.

Stone-Fruit Stew is sweet and delicious eaten on toast or biscuits, and also on top of a scoop of ice cream.

6

AVOCADO
FRUIT of the AZTECS

As a popular fruit, the avocado is in a class by itself. It is neither sweet nor juicy. Nevertheless, it is a delicious fruit, with an unusual nutlike flavor. Avocados are sometimes called "vegetable fruits" and are used more in salads and sandwiches than in desserts.

The avocado is a native American fruit. The trees originated ages and ages ago in Mexico and from there spread southward through Guatemala and other areas of Central and South America.

The Mayan Indian people of ancient Mexico were eating avocados more than two thousand years ago. Later, the Aztec Indians ate avocados, which they mixed with peppers and hot spices. The Aztec word for avocado was *ahuacatl*. In ancient Aztec hieroglyphics, or picture-writing, *ahuacatl* had its own symbol. It was a small drawing of a strange-looking, thick-trunked tree.

In the sixteenth century, Cortez and his soldiers came across the ocean from Spain. They invaded Mexico and conquered the Aztec empire. In the ancient capital city, the conquerors were introduced to the *ahuacatl.* They were probably the first Europeans to see or taste avocados. One man made a study of the strange fruits and of the trees on which they grew. He wrote about them in a report he sent back to his king, Carlos V of Spain. In the report, he called the avocado trees "Aztec pear trees," which were, he wrote, very different from the pear trees of Spain. He also described the fruits and said that they had a strange but delicious flavor, and flesh that was as soft as butter.

In time, the Aztec word, *ahuacatl,* became *aguacate* in Spanish, and, eventually, *avocado* in English. Here are a few of the forty other names the fruit has been called among English-speaking peoples:

custard apple	shell pear
midshipman's butter	butter pear
Spanish pear	vegetable marrow
laurel peach	alligator pear

Some people still use the name "alligator pear," which was first applied to the West Indian avocados because of their dark, bumpy skin like an alligator's hide.

The avocado tree is sub-tropical. That is, it flourishes in regions that border the tropics. It needs a warm, but not extremely hot, climate that is free from severe frost. Through the years since the time of Cortez, young avocado trees have been transported by European planters to various balmy islands and other frost-free areas.

No avocados were grown in the United States until well into the nineteenth century—about three hundred years after Cortez and his men had first tasted the fruit in Mexico. To most people in our country, the avocado was unknown, or was a rare, imported delicacy that only the rich could afford. Then, in 1833, some young avocado trees from Mexico were planted in Florida. And in 1871, there was a planting of Mexican avocados in Santa Barbara, California.

Today, California is the world's leading commercial avocado-growing area. The fruits are also grown in the subtropical regions of Central and South America, Cuba, Israel, South Africa, Hawaii, and Florida. If avocados grow in your state, you may be able to see some of the huge, spreading trees. They are beautiful indeed—thickly covered with clusters of tiny greenish-white blossoms; or weighted down with large, heavy fruits; or just spreading outward with their drooping green branches.

Most avocado trees bear an enormous number of flowers. On a single branch, in space just big enough for two fruits, there may be more than a thousand blossoms! On a typical commercial avocado tree in California, only one flower in more than five thousand develops a seed-bearing fruit. The others just fade and fall from the tree.

Avocado flowers are not easily pollinated, and this is probably why so few of them ever form fruits. Avocado blossoms are small, only about a half inch across when fully open. The pollen is too heavy and too sticky to be carried by small insects, and the flowers are too small and far too many to be hand pollinated. In most areas, honeybees are the best avocado pollinators. They are neither too small nor too large, and they travel from one kind of avocado blossom to another as they gather nectar. The visits of the bees result in cross-pollination.

Most, though not all, avocado trees require cross-pollination in order to develop fruit. They have flowers that encourage cross-pollination and that make self-pollination practically impossible. A flower opens once when its stigma is ready to receive pollen, but its stamens are not shedding pollen. Thus, any pollen that gets to the stigma must come from another flower—usually on another tree. The flower opens a second time, usually the next day, when its stamens are shedding pollen and its stigma is closed. On another tree, the flowers will be following the opposite pattern— opening first to shed pollen and a second time to receive pollen. If cross-pollination is to occur, bees in an avocado orchard must be able to reach both kinds of flowers—on separate trees, or on a single tree where limbs have been added by budding or grafting.

If you can, study a cluster of avocado blossoms through a magnifying glass. Do not pick the cluster, but observe it at different times of the day for several days or longer. Look for one of the tiny flowers that has its vase-shaped

62

stigma erect and ready for pollen. Notice how the closed stamens are flattened out in a circle around the stigma. Look also for flowers when the stamens are open and standing up, ready to shed pollen. With curiosity, patience, and a good magnifying glass, you can get some interesting views of the behavior of blossoms on one kind of flowering tree.

Whether you live in the tropics, sub-tropics, or in the temperate zone where winters are filled with snow and ice, you can grow an avocado tree of your own. You can start it in a jar of water.

AN INDOOR AVOCADO TREE

Save the seed from a fully ripe avocado. Stick the points of three toothpicks into the seed, about halfway between the pointed end and the flat bottom. The toothpicks should be spaced fairly evenly around the seed.

Suspend the flat bottom of the seed in a jar of water. The three toothpicks will serve as supports. Add water as needed to keep the bottom part of the seed wet at all times. If the seed is fully mature, it should sprout in less than thirty days. A "tail"—a thick white root—will push out from the flat bottom, and a green stem with leaves will grow upward from the pointed top. If your seed does not begin to sprout within the thirty-day period, throw it out and start again with a fresh seed.

It is interesting to observe a young avocado tree as it grows and develops in a jar of water. When the seedling tree is about a foot tall and has a good growth of roots, it can be planted in good garden soil in a large flower pot. Keep the soil damp but not muddy, and make sure that the tree gets plenty of light. In the right environment and with proper care, it can become a strong and handsome house plant.

If you live in a warm climate, you can transplant a house-grown avocado tree to the soil outdoors. There, with enough warmth, light, and water, it can grow into a big, handsome tree.

To have enough avocado seeds to experiment with, ask among your relatives and friends to find some who buy and eat avocados. They will probably be glad to save the seeds for you. Look especially for seeds that have already begun to sprout inside fully ripe fruits.

Whether or not you grow any avocado trees, you may enjoy eating the fruits of the ancient Indians. In Guatemala today, the Indian people still say that a good meal is an avocado, four or five tortillas (made of ground-up corn), and a cup of coffee. They are right, for an avocado has many nutritional values. It contains no starch and very little sugar. It is rich in proteins, and contains up to thirty percent of its weight in oil, a kind of oil that is easily digested. It is a good substitute for meat and has the advantage of not having to be cooked. So how about making an avocado burger for your lunch? It will be as delicious and nutritious as a good hot dog or hamburger, or even more so.

Avocado Burger

Peel and cut up a soft, fully ripe avocado. (Don't forget to save the seed to use for sprouting.)

In a bowl, mash the cut-up avocado with a fork. Add from one half to one teaspoonful of fresh lemon juice. If the avocado is a big one, use a full spoonful. Otherwise, use less. Continue to mash and mix with the fork.

Sprinkle the mixture lightly with salt and chile powder. As you mix, take small tastes, adding salt and chile powder in tiny amounts until the seasoning is just right for you.

If you like catsup or tomatoes, add a teaspoonful of catsup or a tablespoonful of cut-up fresh or canned tomato. If you like onions, add a tablespoonful of chopped onions.

Mix well to make a soft, thick paste. Keep tasting and adding to the paste to get the flavor you like. Then spread the avocado paste thickly on toasted white, rye, or whole wheat bread and make sandwiches. Or use the avocado paste as a dip with corn chips, crackers, or sticks of celery.

7

BANANAS, PAPAYAS and MANGOES

IF YOU ENJOY bananas, you are like most people in our country, for Americans are great banana-eaters. In a year we eat more than eleven *billion* of them—an average of about sixty bananas annually for every man, woman, and child in the United States. Yet no bananas are grown here commercially. All eleven billion of them are shipped in each year from other lands.

The banana is one of the oldest fruits known to man. It may have been the first fruit in the world to be cultivated. No one knows for sure, but we do know that words for banana are found in very ancient, almost forgotten languages like Sanskrit and ancient Chinese.

The banana's botanical name, *Musa sapientum*, means "fruit of the wise men." The name derives from an account written by Pliny, a Roman naturalist, about wise men in

India who would sit for days under banana plants, shaded by the broad leaves and fed by the delicious fruits.

When Christianity came to India, old legends located the Garden of Eden in Ceylon, and designated the banana, not the apple, the forbidden fruit which was eaten by Adam and Eve. In the same legends, Adam and Eve made their first garments not from fig leaves, but from banana leaves.

The name "banana" is fairly new in the long history of the fruit. The word is a Portuguese version of a native African name for the fruit.

Bananas probably grew first in the hot, moist valleys of Southeast Asia in prehistoric times. From there they spread around the world, but only in areas that are hot and rainy. Stone Age wanderers carried banana roots to Africa. Arab traders carried them westward to India and the Middle East. Portuguese traders carried them from Africa to the Canary Islands in the Atlantic Ocean. From there, just twenty-five years after Columbus had made his first voyage of discovery, banana plants were brought over to Hispaniola by a missionary priest.

The priest, Friar Tomás de Berlanga, brought an important and lasting gift to the New World, for banana plants spread to all the Caribbean lands, to Mexico, and to Central and South America. In tropical areas, bananas were soon growing on every farm and plantation and in every garden plot, just as they do today. And wherever the banana grows, it is an important source of delicious, nutritious food.

In the United States, however, very few people had ever seen or tasted a banana until about a hundred years ago. Attempts had been made to import bananas, bringing them here on slow sailing ships from banana-growing countries. But in warm weather the fruits had ripened too quickly and spoiled on the way. And in cold weather they froze and turned black.

After many failures, some merchant sea captains learned how to choose bananas that would survive rough seas and long, slow voyages without becoming overripe or badly bruised. Then, as ships became faster, it was less and less difficult to transport bananas successfully. Those that arrived in good condition sold quickly and for high prices. It was obvious from the first that just about everybody liked bananas when they could get them.

Since those early days, many things have changed. Fast steamships with refrigeration speed bananas from tropical lands, where the fruits are raised on plantations, to ports in the United States, Canada, and Europe. From the ports, the bananas travel by truck or train to city markets. Wherever you live, you will find bananas in your neighborhood stores. Unlike apples, peaches, berries, and many other fruits, bananas are always in season. You can buy them all year long.

The next time you eat a banana, notice how easily the skin comes off. This makes the banana an ideal "carry-along" fruit. Its skin can be neatly disposed of in a garbage can or litter basket. All the rest of the fruit can be eaten, for the banana has no core and no seeds.

As you cut or bite into a banana, you may notice the little brown specks in its center. These specks show that once, millions of years ago, bananas did have seeds. They were embedded in the pulp. The fruit is classed as a berry, even though it lost its seed-making ability ages ago. The tiny specks, sometimes referred to as "shadow seeds," are called "vestigial remains" by scientists. Vestigial remains are traces left in a living thing of parts that once grew but are now lost.

A kind of fruit that has no seeds is unusual. How does the plant reproduce—make more plants? For the banana, this is no problem. New plants grow from underground parts called rhizomes. A banana plant becomes twenty to thirty feet tall in a single year. It looks very much like a tree, but what appears to be the trunk is really a roll of tightly wrapped leaves. The banana is the world's tallest kind of plant that has no woody stem, or trunk. The plant's leafy stalk is soft and pithy. A heavy wind can blow down a whole row of the tall plants in a few moments.

The real stem of the banana plant is underground with the roots. The rhizomes are thick, bulblike parts formed by both roots and stem. Each rhizome has many buds. When banana growers set out new plants, they first cut up, then plant the rhizomes, just as farmers cut up and plant potatoes that have "eyes" (buds). The buds of a banana rhizome sprout, grow, and become new plants. They grow very rapidly, as much as an inch a day.

When a banana plant is eight or nine months old, a flower stem grows up from its roots. The stem pushes up through the middle of the hollow stalk and appears at the top. It continues to grow—outward and downward—with a large purple-red bud at the tip. The bud has big, overlapping scales, or bracts. As each bract opens, it reveals a row of small flowers beneath it. The bracts fall, and the flowers develop into clusters, called "hands." Each hand has from ten to twenty "fingers"—the bananas.

As the bananas grow, they turn upward and outward. To us, they seem to grow upside down. Each flower stem will produce about a hundred-and-fifty bananas. The stem is cut while the fruits are still quite green, for bananas ripen better off the plant than on. Only monkeys prefer plant-ripened bananas, which split open and seem mealy and tasteless to us.

A banana plant bears only a single stem of fruit. After the fruits have developed, the plant dies back to the ground or is cut down. Its place is soon taken by several new shoots that spring up from the root parts. Though the above-ground parts of the plant may be dead, the plant has remained alive under ground. Even when rhizomes are dug up and dried out for a long period of time, they still sprout and grow when they are planted and watered. For this reason, it was not hard to transport banana rootstock great distances. Even primitive tribes were able to carry root parts along and plant them in their wanderings.

Wherever bananas grew, they were valued, as they are today. They are not only one of our most nourishing foods, but they are easily digested, delicious, and require no cooking.

More than a thousand years ago, an Arab poet wrote praises of a banana sweet that was popular in Damascus, Cairo, and Constantinople. It was made from bananas, almonds, and honey. You can make and eat your own version of this banana treat of long ago.

HONEY-ALMOND-BANANA CREAM

Peel and mash a fully ripe banana with a fork. Add two teaspoonfuls of honey and mix to make a smooth cream.

Put two or three tablespoonfuls of slivered almonds into a sandwich bag. Crush the almonds by rolling them with a rolling pin. Add the crushed almonds to the honey-banana cream and mix well.

For a special dessert, spread the cream on cookies or

plain cake. Or use the cream as a topping for ice cream or pudding. Or just eat the cream with a spoon.

Special banana drinks are even easier to make. Try this one:

BANANA MILK SHAKE

Peel and mash one banana in a bowl. Add one cupful of cold milk. Beat with an eggbeater until smooth and creamy. Pour into a tall glass, chill, and drink.

For variety, add a tablespoonful of chocolate syrup before beating.

For a delicious, quick-energy lunch, try a new kind of sandwich.

PEANUT BUTTER BANANA SPLIT

Peel a banana and split it in half lengthwise. On one of the cut sides, spread a thick layer of crunchy peanut butter. Press the two banana halves together to form a breadless sandwich. Wrap tightly with aluminum foil. Peel back the foil as you eat.

Two other tropical fruits that are not common here are becoming better known all the time as more fruits travel by air freight. They are the papaya and the mangoe.

The papaya, like the banana, is both abundant and highly prized in the tropics. It began somewhere in the hot areas of this hemisphere, perhaps in Mexico, perhaps in the West Indies. Cortez found papayas being grown by the Aztecs in Mexico. Other Spanish conquerors found them being cultivated by the Incas of Peru in South America.

Papayas are large fruits that weigh up to fifteen pounds each. They look like melons and grow on tall, treelike plants. The big green fruits hang from the plant's trunklike stem, under fans of spreading leaves that crown the top. As the fruit ripens, it turns yellow.

Seeds saved from a ripe papaya can be planted indoors. Those that sprout and grow can be transplanted, one to a pot. With plenty of warmth and moisture, they will grow into handsome house plants. It is important, though, to remember that they are tropical plants and cannot endure chilling or drying out.

In many parts of the world, mangoes are as common as apples and oranges in the United States. Some people find their first taste of mangoes unpleasant. They say that the fruit tastes like turpentine—and some mangoes do. But most good, fully ripe ones have a kind of fruit-salad taste, like a mixture of pineapple, apricot, and peach.

Mangoes are drupe fruits that grow on large, handsome trees. At blossom time, the trees bear clusters of pinkish-white flowers. Later, the ripening fruits dangle from the trees on long stems, like pinkish-orange decorations on a Christmas tree.

Mangoes are very old fruits. They began, as did so many of our fruits, in Southeast Asia. The trees have been cultivated in India for more than four thousand years.

In time, mangoes spread to the West Indies and then to Mexico. Early in the nineteenth century, Mexican mangoes, then varieties from India, were brought to Florida where they are now quite plentiful.

Today, at certain times of the year, both papayas and mangoes are seen in large food markets in many parts of the country. By now Americans have developed a taste for them, especially in fruit salads.

8

PINEAPPLE
KING of FRUITS
FRUIT of KINGS

As WE ALL know, in 1492, on his first voyage of discovery across the unknown ocean-sea, Christopher Columbus discovered the Americas. The following year, when he returned to the New World, he discovered pineapples. He found them being grown by Indians on the island of Guadeloupe in the West Indies.

Columbus carried some of the strange fruits back to Spain and presented them to King Ferdinand and Queen Isabella. A tutor to the royal children happened to be present. He wrote of watching the king as he tasted the new fruit, only one of which was still good after the long ocean voyage.

The pineapple that King Ferdinand bit into was probably small, tough, fibrous, and more acid than sweet. It may also have been filled with seeds like small apple seeds. We

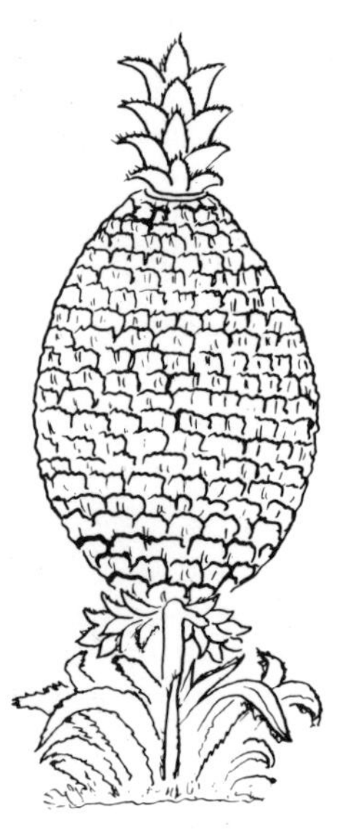

know that it could not have been much like the large, succulent pineapples we have today. Nevertheless, according to the tutor's account, the king was delighted with the fruit's unusual flavor and fragrance. Word of the new fruit soon spread from Spain to the other countries of Europe. Pineapple was a success!

Explorers who came after Columbus studied pineapple plants, wrote scientific descriptions of them, and illustrated their accounts with drawings of the fruits. The earliest of these is in a history of the Indies, written in Spanish in 1520.

The rare, handsome fruit from far away became a symbol of hospitality. Artists and craftsmen used it as a decorative motif on fine china, silverware, and carved furniture. With its crown of stiff, spiky leaves, the "king of fruits" was known for several hundred years to people who had never tasted or even seen real pineapples, for they could not be grown in the European climate.

Pineapples are tropical plants and can grow only where the weather is warm all year long. They are native South Americans. They probably began in regions that are now Brazil and Paraguay, where the Indians had long used them as medicinal plants for treating a variety of diseases. The pineapples that Columbus discovered had been brought to the island of Guadeloupe, by way of Panama, following the paths of conquest of an ancient tribe of Guarani Indians. The ancestors of today's cultivated pineapples were proba-

bly like some of the wild ones that can still be found in Brazil. Their fruits are small and their long, slender leaves are tough, with sharp hooks along the edges.

European explorers after the time of Columbus spread pineapples through tropical lands beyond the Americas. Although ripe fruits spoiled during long voyages, whole plants, and also slips and suckers from plants, traveled successfully to distant places on the sailing ships of the 1500's. Thus pineapple-growing spread from island to island and from continent to continent all around the world—the East Indies, China, India, and tropical Africa.

In 1657, a group of Englishmen returned home from a business trip to China with four pineapple plants. They presented the fruits to Oliver Cromwell, who was then the ruler of England. By the end of the same century, ripe pineapples were being grown in England. They were being grown under glass.

Until the end of the seventeenth century, greenhouses had not been practical because window glass had been too scarce and costly to be used for gardening. For hundreds of years only the very wealthiest people ever had glass windows in their homes. When the first greenhouses were built, they were expensive luxuries, found only in the gardens of kings and on the estates of the richest noblemen.

On cold days and nights, these early greenhouses were heated by specially designed stoves with towering chimneys. On warm, sunny days, they were heated as our greenhouses are heated today. Sunlight shines through the glass, and heat from the sunlight is trapped and held inside. A tropical climate is thus artificially created for the growing of tropical plants.

The first English-grown pineapple was presented to King Charles II by his royal gardener. So important was the event that a painting was made showing the handsome king, in his elegant royal robes and with his two favorite pet dogs, receiving a rather puny little pineapple. From then on, pineapples were grown and ripened under glass as highly prized luxuries for the tables of kings.

The ancient Guarani Indians, who were probably the first to cultivate the pineapple, called it *anana*, from a Guarani word for fragrance. In most European languages, the word for pineapple is still *anana*, or a word much like it. If you

want to buy a pineapple in France, Germany, or Portugal, ask for *ananas*. In Italy, ask for *ananasso*. In Spain or Mexico, ask for *anana* or for *piña*. Our English word came from the name that was given to the fruit by very early Spanish explorers. They noticed the pine-cone-shaped fruits and called them *"piñas de los Indies"*—pine cones of the Indies. We call them pine-cone apples, for the word apple was often used in the past as a general term for fruit.

Today, pineapples are cultivated in most tropical lands, and especially in our own state of Hawaii, where a very large percentage of the world's supply is now grown. No one knows exactly how or when the first pineapples came to Hawaii. All we can be sure of is that pineapples were being grown there by 1813, which was rather late in the history of pineapple growing.

During the California Gold Rush of 1849, fresh ripe pine-apples were shipped from Hawaii all the way to San Francisco to the Forty-niners, who often had plenty of gold and were eager to spend some of it on the luxuries they craved. Some of the pineapples from the Islands were still edible when they arrived, but many of them had spoiled during the long trip across the Pacific Ocean.

In Hawaii pineapple growers realized that the fruits would have to be canned if they were to be shipped successfully. Experiments began. Two men cooked up a small amount of the fruit on a kitchen stove and then sealed it in homemade cans. Others tried canning pineapples in tin and in glass containers. These early trials were not especially successful, but they prepared the way for the big pineapple industry of today, which now includes miles of plantations, can factories, research stations, laboratories, office buildings, shipping facilities, and canneries, including the biggest fruit cannery in the world.

Of all our popular fruits, pineapple probably loses least of its true fresh flavor and texture when canned. All over the world people are now enjoying canned pineapple and pineapple juice. And, because of today's fast ships and faster planes, markets in most of our cities carry freshly picked pineapples that are almost as sweet and delicious as those sold in Hawaii.

As you look at a pineapple's crown of stiff green leaves, you see why it is still called the king of fruits. But it is no longer a fruit mainly for kings. Fresh, canned, or frozen, it is now eaten and enjoyed by millions of people.

Pineapples are different from most other fruits. They do not grow on trees, bushes, or vines but on rather low plants that are pulled up and replaced every few years. The pineapple is a bromeliad and has some peculiar-looking relatives. One of these is Spanish moss, the gray-green stuff we see hanging like tattered curtains from trees in warm southern states. Spanish moss is not moss at all, for it has tiny roots, stems, leaves, and flowers, which you can see through an ordinary magnifying glass. Like the typical bromeliad, Spanish moss is an aerial plant, supported by a tree or vine. Its roots are in the air, and its leaves collect and hold water from rain.

Pineapple plants, however, are rooted in soil. They have woody underground roots and also little air roots, which grow in pockets formed by overlapping leaves. The leaves of the plant are sharp, swordlike, and bluish green. They grow outward from a thick, fibrous stem. The fruit, which develops at the top of the stem, is a multiple fruit. This means that it is made up of many small fruits grown together and attached to a central core. Each of the "eyes" you see on the skin of a pineapple marks a separate little fruit that developed from a separate flower. Since these small fruitlets ripen one by one over a period of time, there is no such thing as a completely ripe pineapple. Before the last little fruit is fully ripe, the first ones are overripe. So, in picking out a ripe pineapple it is always necessary to compromise between the overripe and the underripe fruitlets in order to get a fruit without too many of either.

At the top of the fruit is the crown of leaves. A whole new plant can be grown from the crown, as well as from a slip at the base of the fruit, or from a sucker at the base of the plant.

The thick part of the stem holds the plant's starch reserve. During the last stage of ripening, starch in the stem changes to sugar and moves upward into the fruit. The lower part sweetens first and most, and the upper part is always less sweet. The fruit itself has no starch at any stage. Many

people do not know that once a pineapple has been picked it can never become any sweeter. Cut from its stem, it is separated from its only source of additional sugar. In this respect, pineapples are different from apples, pears, and many other fruits that can be picked somewhat green and left to ripen and sweeten off the mother plant.

Color does not always show a pineapple's sweetness. Some sweet, fully ripe fruits are golden yellow, and some are partly green. Fragrance, more than color, indicates the degree of ripeness. To select a good pineapple, use your nose as a ripeness detector.

86

Pineapple, King of Fruits

It takes about twenty months for a pineapple plant to produce its first ripe fruit. This is called the "plant crop." Each plant bears just one fruit and it is the largest it will ever bear. After the plant crop has been picked, workers remove the slips and perhaps take off some of the suckers. One or two suckers are left on each plant to produce the next year's fruit, called the "ratoon crop." This time, each plant bears two, or even three, fruits, but they are much smaller than plant-crop fruits. The plants would continue to bear year after year, but each year the fruits would be smaller. On most commercial plantations, the plants are pulled up after the ratoon crop. This means that each plant usually produces only three or four pineapples. Then the area is cleared for replanting.

New plantings are watched over and cared for as they grow. When a plant is about fifteen months old, it has a little flower bud that looks like a small pinkish artichoke or pine cone. When this is several inches long, little tubelike purple-blue flowers begin to appear, the first ones at the base. Each flower is open for a single day. The flowering continues for a couple of weeks, blossom by blossom in a spiral pattern from bottom to top of the bud.

Pineapple flowers are not self-pollinating, and neither wind nor small insects can do the job. Hummingbirds, with their long bills and longer tongues, can do it easily. However, there are few if any hummingbirds in Hawaii, and it is said to be against Hawaiian law to bring any of them to the Islands. Except as a result of an occasional visit by an unusually large bee, plants on commercial plantations in Hawaii are not pollinated, and the fruits are usually seedless.

About twenty months from the time of planting, the plants are three feet high and fully mature. Each bears a single large pineapple, the plant crop, ready to be picked.

The best pineapple in the world is Hawaiian pineapple—*if* you are used to eating Hawaiian pineapple. But if you are an African or a Mexican, you probably prefer the kind grown in Africa or Mexico. Travelers who have tasted pineapples from many lands agree that they are all delicious. Nevertheless, pineapple growers are never satisfied. They work continuously to develop new species.

New species of pineapple are developed by cross-pollinating. This is done by skilled workers who carefully brush pollen-filled stamens from one species onto the pistils of flowers of another species. This results in pineapples with seeds.

Plants grown from the seeds are hybrids, which may be quite different from either of the parent species. Sometimes a hybrid has the worst traits of both parents. Sometimes it has the best. When the latter occurs, more plants that are exactly like the hybrid are grown from the plant's suckers, shoots, and the crowns of its fruits. Even half or a quarter of one of these parts can produce a true copy of the hybrid plant on which it grew.

Season after season and year after year, in research stations in various parts of the world, the work of hybridizing goes on in efforts to develop the perfect pineapple. Or at least to produce new species that resist pests and diseases, bear fruits that are neither too firm nor too soft, neither too sweet nor too tart, and that are even more fragrant and delicious than those grown today.

This is all part of the unending work of men and women who study and work with plants, looking after and improving the ones that produce the foods on which we depend.

GROW A PINEAPPLE PLANT OF YOUR OWN

Even if you live where the winters are cold, you can grow your own pineapple plants. You can see for yourself how easy it is to grow a new plant from a crown.

Twist off the crown of a fresh pineapple from your neighborhood food market. Eat the luscious fruit for dessert and use the crown to start a bromeliad plant that will grow well indoors.

Strip off some of the bottom leaves to expose about an inch of the thick stem. You will see small white bumps on the stem. These are little root eyes.

Put the crown in a jar or vase, with enough water to cover the bottom inch of stem. Keep the jar on a windowsill or in some other sunny, warm place. Watch it each day, adding water as needed to keep the stem wet. In a short time, often in less than a week, white roots from the root eyes will be growing out on all sides.

When the roots are a few inches long, you may want to plant the crown in good soil in a clay flower pot. Then root a second crown and keep this one growing in water, comparing the two plants as they grow. It is not hard to grow real pineapple plants at home if you remember that they are tropical plants. They can be moved outdoors each year for the warm months, but they must be brought back indoors to a warm place before the cold days of autumn.

In water or soil, pineapples make handsome and interesting house plants. Those in soil, if well cared for, will even produce little fruits that are as sweet and delicious as the big ones that grow in Hawaii.

9

FIGS and their MYSTERIOUS FLOWERS

HAVE YOU EVER tasted a fresh fig? Dried figs? Canned ones? Or fruit-filled fig-bar cookies?

Most Americans have eaten dried Smyrna, Calimyrna, or Mission figs. Canned Kadota figs are on the shelves of most food markets. Few of us, however, are familiar with fresh figs unless we live in an area where fig trees grow. Unlike many of our delicious fruits, figs are allowed to ripen fully on the tree. Those to be dried stay on until they fall to the ground. Then they are gathered, cleaned, and dried carefully in the sun.

The plump, luscious ripe figs are so thin-skinned and tender that packing and shipping them to distant markets is a delicate and costly procedure. Most figs, therefore, are dried or canned before they reach us. But people in fig country say that there are few things more delicious for dessert than sliced raw figs and cream.

Fig trees probably originated in Asiatic Turkey and northern India. From there, in prehistoric times, they moved to Israel and the Near East and then to all areas around the Mediterranean. Fossils in rock layers show that figlike plants were growing in southern Europe long before the Stone Age.

The fig tree was important in many ancient cultures. The Hebrews referred to it many times in Old Testament writings. The Ancient Egyptians painted pictures of fig trees on tomb walls in the pyramids. Wood from fig trees was often used for Egyptian masks and mummy cases.

The ancient Greeks treasured the fig tree and honored it. According to one of their legends, the first fig tree in the world sprang from a thunderbolt flung by the god, Jupiter. Fig trees figured in the tales of Homer and in the writings of Plato.

In ancient Rome, the fig was believed to be sacred, a gift from the god Bacchus, and was used in religious ceremonies. Even today, having a fig tree of one's own, spreading its branches and bearing its fruits in one's own dooryard, is looked upon by many people as a symbol of prosperity.

Like many fruits that began in eastern lands, figs were brought to North America from Spain. Before the end of the 1500's, fig trees were flourishing in St. Augustine, Florida. Today, most of our country's commercial fig growing is in California, where the first trees were planted at the

mission in San Diego in 1750. These were the purplish, almost black figs that we now call Mission figs.

Fig trees are sometimes called "flowerless fruit trees." It is true that we never see fig trees in bloom. Nevertheless, they have thousands of flowers, small and unseen. They grow *inside* the fruits, which are really hollow pouches—the enlarged ends of flower stalks. When flowering time is over, tiny hard seeds develop, each one covered by a small fleshy fruit. So, when we eat a dried, canned, or fresh fig, we are really eating many tiny fruits and their seeds, plus the baglike container in which they have grown.

Cut open a fig and, using a magnifying glass, take a good look at its inside parts. Imagine what the inside is like when it is filled, not with little fruits, but with tiny flowers.

Many varieties of fig trees do not need pollination in order to bear good fruits. The seeds in such fruits are hollow and undeveloped. New trees are started, not from fig seeds, but from branches cut from mature trees. A branch roots easily and in only a few years becomes a full-grown tree.

One of the world's important varieties, the Smyrna, is used mainly for dried figs. Smyrnas grown in California are called Calimyrna figs. They did not get their start in this country until late in the 1800's. The story of the Smyrna fig is one of the wonder tales of natural history.

The first Californians to plant this variety did not know that the Smyrnas contained only female flowers and that they had to be pollinated with pollen from another kind of fig. In the first California orchards, the trees flourished and produced small green figs, which shriveled and fell, unripe, to the ground. When this happened year after year, growers began to despair. Most of them blamed the climate. California, they thought, was too hot, too cold, too wet, or too dry for Smyrna figs, which grew so well in Turkey and Greece.

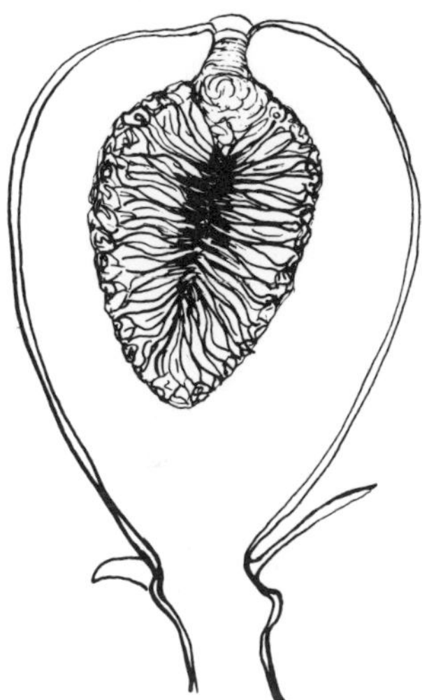

A few growers, however, began to pay attention to an old rumor—a rumor that some kind of small insect was needed to pollinate the Smyrnas with pollen from wild figs. Some growers made investigations and secured cuttings of wild fig trees, called caprifigs. But the Americans were not able to get any of the little insects. Nevertheless, two growers pollinated their Smyrnas by hand, using pollen from the caprifigs. This was a slow and tedious process, but the luscious, fully developed fruits that resulted proved that caprifig pollen was essential.

In Greece, Turkey, and other countries where Smyrna figs grew well, the growers did not have to do the pollinating by hand. They had the *Blastophaga*, the tiny fig wasp, to do the job. The prosperous growers were shipping their delicious dried Smyrna figs to markets all over the world. Understandably, they were not eager to send any of their own little wasps to California to help develop new competition.

Finally, in 1899, the United States Department of Agriculture became involved. It was able to secure some of the

Blastophaga wasps for the American fig orchards. The tiny insects seemed to be true partners of fig trees, especially Smyrnas, whose flowers must be pollinated.

The complex process of pollination begins when a female wasp enters a caprifig through a small hole in the middle of the flat, wide end. A caprifig contains both male flowers (with stamens and pollen) and female flowers (with pistils). The pollen-bearing male flowers are near the entrance hole. As the wasp enters the fig, it makes its way over the male flowers to the other end of the fruit and lays its eggs among the female flowers. The eggs act as irritants to the plant tissue, and small tumorlike growths, called galls, form around them. The galls serve as incubators in which the tiny eggs pass from stage to stage—to larvae, to pupae, and then to adults—each in its own little gall.

Some of the adults are females with wings and the rest are wingless males. An adult male makes a hole in its gall, crawls out, and somehow finds a gall that encloses a female. The male makes a hole in the female's gall and crawls in. The wasps mate, and the female then works itself out of the gall, leaving the male to die. Its entire short life has been spent in darkness inside the caprifig.

The female, however, has things to do. It makes its way through the pollen-filled male flowers, out of the caprifig and into the open air. Its body now laden with grains of pollen, the little wasp opens its wings and flies off in search of a suitable place to lay its eggs. For reasons not fully understood, the wasp goes, not to a caprifig, but to Smyrna figs, crawling in and out, brushing against the pistils of the female flowers. A wasp will enter one fig after another and walk around among the flowers. It seems to want to settle down and lay its eggs, but it cannot find a suitable place because of the Smyrna flowers' very tall pistils. In its vain attempts at egg laying, one Blastophaga pollinates many edible figs with pollen from the wild and inedible caprifig.

Finally, the little insect seems to give up. It seeks out a caprifig that is ready, crawls in through its tiny entrance hole, and the entire process, called "caprification," begins again.

Once a Smyrna fig has been pollinated, a kind of seal grows over its entrance hole. Then the seeds develop and the fruits form. Later, as the ripe figs are dried, the seal breaks open.

Long ago, the Greeks, Romans, and other ancient peoples knew about caprification. Some cut fruit-bearing branches from caprifig trees and hung them in their orchards. Some grafted branches of the wild fig onto trees that bore edible fruits. Others planted a few caprifig trees in their fig orchards.

To people in Mediterranean lands figs were, and still are, a very important food. They are high in food energy and delicious in taste. In this country dried figs are commonly used in cookies, candies, puddings, fruit cakes, and other desserts, especially at holiday time. Dried figs are good for

after-school snacks and in sandwiches any time of the year.

CALIFORNIA FIG SANDWICHES

Spread two slices of your favorite kind of bread thickly with crunchy peanut butter. Cut dried figs into small bits and press them into the peanut butter. Sprinkle lightly with brown sugar.

Put the two slices of bread together with the thick, crunchy-chewy filling inside. Cut into four square sandwiches. These will serve two people—or one very hungry one.

10

DATES
FRUIT of the DESERT

THE DATE PALM is a tall tree whose unbranched stem goes straight up to its handsome crown of leaves. The long, graceful leaves spread out from the top like giant green feathers. Jews, Christians, and many ancient peoples before them have used palm leaves in their religious services.

Desert dwellers have long held the date palm as sacred, and for very good reason. In countries with thousands of miles of barren sand, date palms have been great providers since long before Bible times. The living trees have offered welcome shade from the burning sun. The fruits, with their high sugar content, have provided an important food. The dried palm leaves have been useful in making mats, baskets, and bags. Palm fiber has been twisted into rope. The buds were sometimes picked and eaten as vegetables. The fruit pits have been roasted and used as a substitute for coffee, or ground up and pressed to yield oil. And any left-over materials could always be used as fodder for animals, or as fuel for fire in otherwise treeless lands.

Date palms grow naturally in hot deserts, especially around an oasis, where water from springs soaks through the soil. Roots of the palm trees grow deep into the ground and can reach moisture far below the surface. The trees can thrive in hot, sandy regions where rain seldom falls, though only where there is plenty of underground moisture.

Commercial date growers irrigate the soil to provide water for the roots. Water soaked in by the roots moves upward to all parts of the trees. Though date palms need

much soil water, they can be damaged by rain. Even a light rainfall while the fruits are ripening can make them moldy and sour. Hence, dates are usually grown where there is no danger of rain throughout summer and fall.

Freshly picked dates, like freshly picked figs, are not commonly known in our country, except in areas where the fruits are actually grown. California cultivates most of our home-grown dates. Arizona and Texas grow some too. However, at least three-fourths of the world's dates are grown in Iraq, in land where date palms have been flourishing for thousands of years.

New date palms are started by planting shoots cut from the base of superior trees when they are three to five years old. When carefully watered and tended, the shoots grow to be superior trees like the parent palms. A date seed can also be planted, and a new tree will grow from it. The new tree, however, will be a new variety, usually inferior to the parent tree. Therefore, the only sure way to reproduce a superior variety is to plant the offshoots of superior trees.

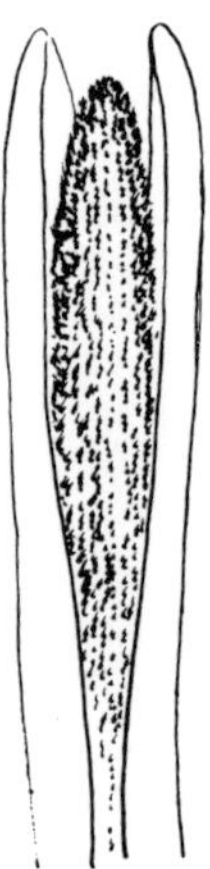

Most fruit trees are neither male nor female. Their flowers, apple blossoms, for example, have both male parts (pollen-bearing .stamens) and female parts (pistil with ovule-bearing ovary). Some date palms, however, are female trees and some are male. Female trees have only female offshoots and female flowers. Likewise, the offshoots and flowers of male trees are male.

Only the male flowers, called *staminate* flowers, have pol-

102

len. Only the female, or *pistillate*, flowers can form fruits. But to do so, they must be pollinated with pollen from male flowers, which grow only on male trees. Since only the male flowers have fragrance and attract insects, bees do not carry pollen to the female flowers.

Where date palms grow wild, there are about as many male trees as female ones. In these areas, the wind transfers pollen from male to female. In commercial date groves, however, there may be fifty to a hundred female trees to every male tree, and the pollinating is accomplished entirely by hand. This is usually done by tying little bunches of male flowers onto each cluster of female flowers. The process may have to be repeated several times because not all of the separate flowers in the female cluster mature at the same time.

In the big date groves near Indio, California, hand pollinating begins in February and continues until May. Then, as the fruits ripen, each cluster is covered with a large paper bag to protect it from birds and insects and from any rain that might happen to fall. The individual dates in each cluster ripen at different times. The picking, like the pollinating, goes on for months—from September through December.

There are three main varieties of dates: soft, semidry, and dry. Soft dates are seldom shipped to markets, but are most often used in making candies and cookies. The semidry are those most commonly found in our stores. The dry dates, which are rarely grown or sold in the United

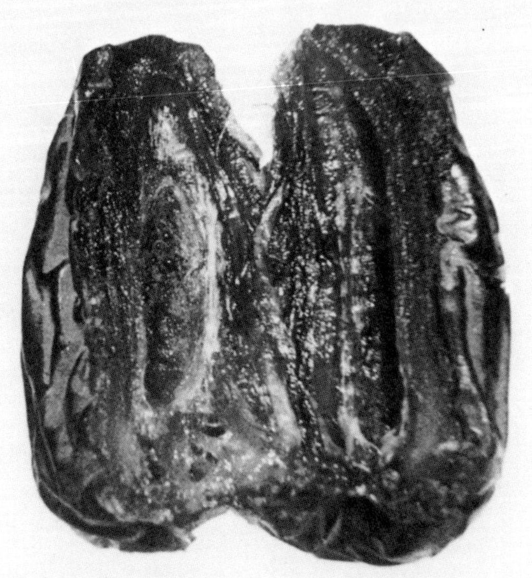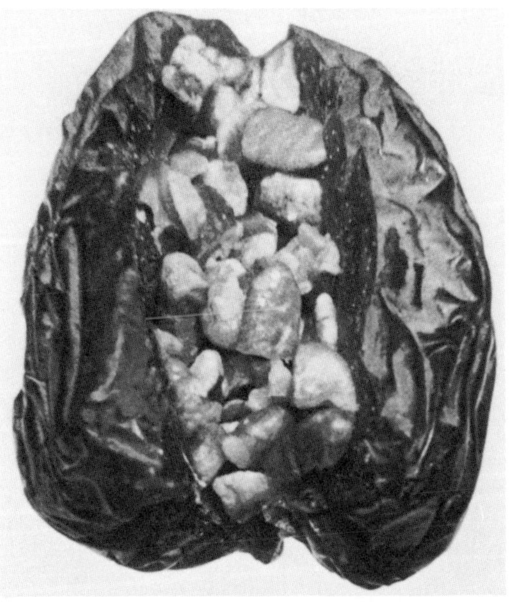

States, are very sweet, hard, and lasting. This kind is an important food in Arab countries.

For a treat or a snack, sweet, chewy dates are better than candy. To make them even more delicious, follow the recipe below.

SUGARY STUFFED DATES

Split open a dozen dates and remove the pits. Fill the cavities with pieces of walnuts, almonds, or pecans. Pull each date together to cover the nuts.

Spread a layer of granulated sugar on a plate. Roll each stuffed date in the sugar until it is well coated on all sides. Then arrange the sugary dates on a clean plate, or wrap each one in a square of waxed paper.

Eat Sugary Stuffed Dates in place of candy. Or pack paper-wrapped ones in a box or jar for a delicious home-made gift.

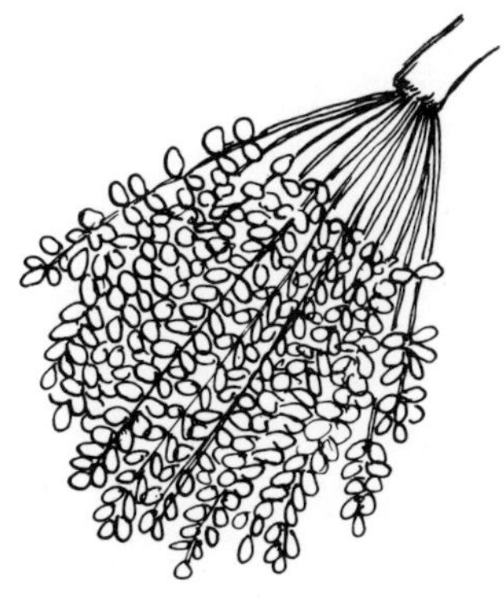

11

BERRIES
LARGE and SMALL

A BERRY MAY be as big as the world's biggest watermelon, or as small as the tiniest gooseberry that ever hung from a bush. Its skin may be red, orange, yellow, green, blue, purple, or almost black. It may grow on a tree, on a bush, or on a vine.

Some of the fruits we call berries are not berries at all. And some, like oranges, which we never think of as berries, really are. To the botanist, a berry is a fruit with pulpy flesh that holds seeds which have no stony covering, all enclosed in a rind or skin. Melons, then, are berries. And so are grapes. So are cranberries, blueberries, currants, and gooseberries. Raspberries and blackberries, however, are not true berries, and neither are strawberries!

Melons belong to the *cucurbit* family, the plant family of the cucumbers and squashes we eat as vegetables. All of them grow on vines (plants with long, trailing stems).

Berries Large and Small

Watermelons originated in Africa, where they have been cultivated as a garden crop for thousands of years. The vines are planted in relatively dry soil, and in years of heavy rainfall they spread out and cover large areas. The juicy fruits, ripened by the hot African sun, are then enjoyed, not only by the natives, but also by wandering animals, from elephants to field mice, and by some of the flesh-eaters too.

From Africa watermelons spread to Asia, southern Europe, and eventually to the Americas. As early as 1629, colonists in Massachusetts were enjoying their own home-grown watermelons. And by 1799 Indians were raising them as far west as the Colorado River.

For the early American settlers, and also for the Indians,

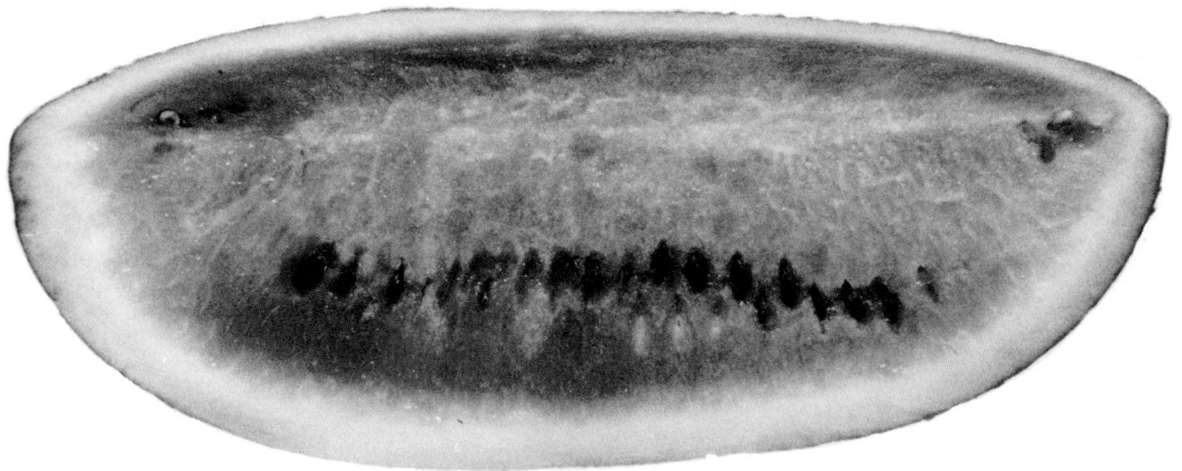

watermelons were convenient, time-saving fruits. Unlike apples and other tree fruits, watermelons are planted, grown, ripened, and harvested in a single growing season. The vines are annuals; they are grown each year from seed.

Today, Florida, Texas, and Georgia are our leading watermelon-growing states—all in the warmer areas of our country. However, some watermelons are grown in all states, as far north as Canada. The seeds are not planted until summer weather has already begun. The fruits are then ripe in about eighty-five days. With melons, there is no waiting for five or six years until the plant matures and begins to bear fruits.

A mouthful of cold, crisp, juicy watermelon on a hot afternoon is one of nature's most refreshing treats. As the fruit's name indicates, it is mainly water (93 percent water). But the water is sweet, and the flavor is delicious—better than any drink you can make or buy.

Muskmelons are our other most popular melons. They probably began in India, but spread in very early times from that country to other areas of tropical Asia, Africa, and the East Indies. Muskmelons were grown by the ancient Greeks and Romans and by later Europeans. Since Colonial times, they have been cultivated in America.

Like watermelons, muskmelons are grown only in the warm summer months. The seeds are planted in little mounds, and the long, trailing vines spread out in all directions. Each vine has two kinds of flowers: small male (sta-

108

minate) flowers, and larger female (pistillate) flowers. There are many of the pollen-bearing staminate flowers to each pistillate one. This helps to assure pollination, most of which is done by insects. After pollination, the staminate flowers wither and fall from the vine, and the pistillate flowers then form fruits.

Muskmelons were named for their strong scent, which reminds some people of musk, an oily substance produced by glands of certain wild animals. Some kinds of muskmelons do have a strong odor, but many kinds do not. Persian, honeydew, casaba, and other "winter melons" are different varieties of muskmelon.

The cantaloupe is also a kind of muskmelon. It was named for Cantalupo, Italy, a town near Rome where the first European ones were grown. About 1890, some were shipped from Cantalupo to the United States. A true cantaloupe has a hard, fibrous outer skin and deep orange-colored pulp. It is a tough fruit that can endure transoceanic or cross-country shipping without injury. Other varieties of muskmelon have smoother, softer skin, and are more delicate than the rugged cantaloupe.

Grapes, like melons, are berries, though we do not ordinarily think of them as such. But, as you bite into one and feel the seeds embedded in the pulp, you can tell at once that is is truly a berry.

In prehistoric times, people gathered the grapes that grew wild on the vines. By the dawn of history, people were planting their own vinyards, tending their own vines, and making their own wine from their own grapes.

Grape vines have been on the earth for so long, and have been so widespread since such very early times, that we cannot tell when and where they originated. However, prehistoric grapes left their traces in Bronze Age villages in Europe, in ancient tombs in Egypt, and in the oldest writings of the Hebrews, Greeks, and Romans.

The Norsemen, as you know, were the first Europeans to land on the shores of North America. When they arrived, in about the year 1000, they found so many wild grape vines that they named the land Vinland. Hundreds of years later, when the English settlers arrived in Virginia, they found old grape vines festooned from the trees. They spoke of this land as a "vineyard paradise," and set about to improve the quality of the wild grapes of the New World.

The American wild grapes could not compare with the best of the wine grapes then being grown in Europe. The first step to improve the American stock was to import some superior vines from the great vinyards of the Old World. Another step was the passing of laws that encouraged grape growing in all of the colonies. A third step was to promise rewards to people who succeeded in growing good grapes and making good wine, with penalties for those who refused to try.

The colonists worked hard. They tried. And they failed. Because of insect pests and fungus diseases, grapes from the Old World did not grow well in eastern North Ameica.

In the West, however, things were different. The Spanish, who had founded a colony in New Mexico as early as 1598, had planted grapevines. Then, beginning in 1769, Spanish padres established the missions in California and planted grapes. In the milder, dryer climate of the Southwest, the Old World grapes made themselves at home and flourished, and they continue to flourish to this day.

Grapevines are hardy, woody plants. Their bark-covered trunks are often gnarled and twisted with age. Their main branches, called "arms," may spread out as much as a hundred feet. New growths, which are soft and green, turn brown when they drop their leaves in the fall. They are then called "canes." Twelve-inch pieces of cane are cut, stored through the winter, and planted early in spring to start new grapevines.

Old grapevines, which have been bare all winter, put out new green leaves in spring. Then come flower stems with bunches of little flowers, followed by tiny green fruits that look like clusters of beads. The fruits grow and ripen in the summer sun, forming bunches of red, blue, purple, or golden-green grapes.

By now, native American species, which grow well in eastern states, have been improved through years of cultivation. Careful selection and cross-breeding have resulted in the choice grapes used for grape juice, jams, and jellies.

Most of the Old World grapes that are grown so success-

fully in California vinyards are used in wine-making. World wide, grape growing is the biggest of all fruit industries, and has been for a very long time. Today, as in all past ages, most of the world's grapes are used for wine. The second largest portion supplies the raisin industry.

Since ancient times, grapes have been dried in the sun and used as raisins. The ancient Egyptians ate them, and so did the Israelites, the Romans, the Greeks, and other long-ago peoples. But for centuries, raisins were a luxury food and only the very wealthy could afford them. Today, a small box of raisins costs only a few cents, and they are favorite treats for children everywhere.

There are four main kinds of raisin grapes. The Thompson seedless are made into the familiar little seedless raisins we buy in small or large boxes. Seed-bearing Muskat grapes, first brought to California by the mission padres, are dried to become the large, soft, somewhat seedy raisins that are sticky to handle. Sultanas are made into pale golden raisins that have a special flavor. And the little Corinthian grapes become the tiny dark raisins that are sold as currants and used in cinnamon buns, fruit cakes, and other baked goods.

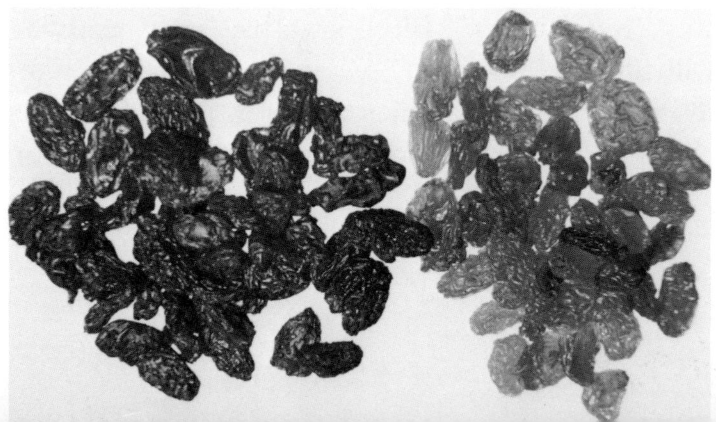

For raisin grapes, the rows of vines are planted far apart. The grapes ripen fully on the vines and are then picked by hand. The bunches are placed on shallow trays or on pieces of brown paper on the ground, between the rows of vines. There they dry in the sun for from ten to fifteen days. They are then stacked, and allowed to "sweat" to equalize the moisture. After that, they are sent to packing houses for stemming, grading, washing and cleaning, and packing.

When you eat a dozen raisins, you are really eating a dozen grapes in concentrated form. Most of the water has been removed in the sun-drying process, and the sugar content has increased. The raisins contain important vitamins and minerals, as well as easily digested sugar for quick energy. How wonderful that a food that tastes so delicious is also good for us!

Another kind of fruit which is good for us did not taste good at all to the early settlers when they first tried it. When the Pilgrims arrived on the coast of Massachusetts they found strange, bitter berries growing in swampy land. They did not know what to do with them, until they learned about them from the Indians.

In some tribes, the Indian name for the fruit is I-bimi, meaning "bitter berry." Bite into a fresh raw cranberry and you will quickly discover how it got its Indian name. The Indians used the red berries as food, pounding them into dried deer meat and fat to make pemmican, a nourishing,

114

long-lasting food that was handy for traveling. The medicine men used the mashed berries on wounds, to prevent blood poisoning, they believed. Indian women used cranberry juice as a dye, something you may enjoy trying.

CRANBERRY DYE

Boil a handerchief, bit of white yarn, or any scrap of cotton or wool in cranberry juice, or in the juice of some mashed fresh cranberries. Boil until the material is as pink as you wish. Then take the pan off the stove. When pan and contents are cool, remove the material and spread it on paper towels to dry.

In time, the Pilgrims began to use the red berries from the bogs as food. They called them "crane berries," because the vines' flowers looked to them like heads of wild cranes. Later, the name was contracted to cranberry. There is no evidence that cranberries were served with the turkey and bear meat at the first Thanksgiving dinner. But we do know that there was much picking, trading, and eating of wild cranberries in the early years of colonization.

Cranberries are native from North Carolina northward to Nova Scotia in Canada, and eastward to Wisconsin. The vines are found mainly in low, swampy land that floods in winter and drains in summer. In Colonial days, the Cape Cod region of Massachusetts was especially rich in cranberries, and it still is today. Now, however, we no longer have

115

to depend on wild berries. We have an extensive and highly skilled cranberry industry, with vines in specially built bogs that can be flooded and drained quickly.

In Colonial times, and for many years after, ripe berries were picked by combing through the vines with toothed cranberry scoops made of wood. Some of these can still be found in antique shops, especially in New England.

Today, most cranberry picking is done by gasoline-powered machines that are rolled over the vines like a big lawnmower, or by huge vacuum machines with suction hoses that draw the ripe berries off the vines. Some growers, though, do what is called "wet harvesting." They flood the bogs, then make waves with a machine called an "eggbeater." Ripe berries, shaken off the vines by the waves, are floated along on top of the water and are then scooped up.

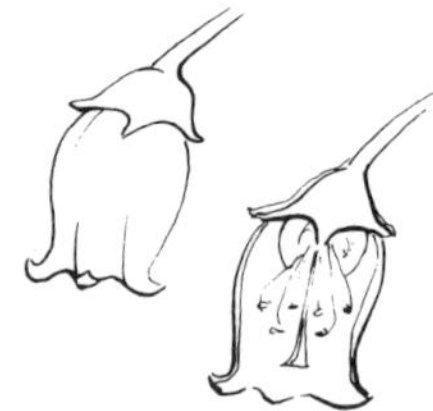

Most of today's enormous cranberry harvest is used for canning—cranberry sauce and cranberry juice. The rest is sold raw, mainly during the Thanksgiving and Christmas seasons.

Blueberries, which are also native Americans, may be the world's most widely distributed fruits. They seem to have been native to most of the northern regions of the earth, and can still be found in their wild state from tropical to arctic lands. The plants are easily grown. They reseed themselves and require very little care.

In America, blueberries grow wild as far north as northern Alaska and Canada, where they have long been important in the diet of Eskimo people. A few years ago, Eskimo children in a school in the Far North collected recipes of their favorite dishes for a booklet they were making. Here is one of their recipes.

ESKIMO BLUEBERRY DESSERT

Fill a bowl with fresh snow. Add some mashed blueberries and some soft seal blubber. Mix well. Set it outdoors to chill, then eat.

You probably have no seal blubber, and you might not like the taste of it if you had. But for children of the Arctic, rich fat from a seal is a treat, just as rich cream from a cow is a treat for you.

BLUEBERRY ICE CREAM

Put one pint of vanilla ice cream into a bowl and let it get slightly soft. Add one cupful of washed and dried blueberries—fresh ones or unsweetened frozen ones. Use a large spoon to stir and to work the berries into the ice cream.

Take enough out for a generous taste, then spoon the rest of the mixture into freezer trays or pans. Cover with foil or plastic wrap and put into the freezer to harden.

Huckleberries are close relatives of blueberries, but do not have the silvery, dusty-looking "bloom" found on blue-

berry skin. Most of them are dark blue and very shiny, and contain fairly large, stony seeds. Though they look like true berries, huckleberries are classed as drupes, or stone fruits.

When you look at the thorny bramble bushes on which raspberries and blackberries grow, you are not surprised that they are members of the Rose family. An open blossom looks a little like a white wild rose.

Raspberries and blackberries are classed as aggregate fruits. Each one is a collection of many separate little fruitlets around a central core. The seeds are inside the fruitlets, which are tiny drupe fruits. These and other bramble fruits are native to Asia, Europe, and North America. They spring up in neglected fields and spread out over dead brush and other rubbish. For a long time there were so many of the wild bramble fruits that there was no need to cultivate them.

When the first settlers arrived here, they found both red and black raspberries growing wild. Our modern raspberries are all hybrids of native American species and those brought here from Europe.

When a raspberry is picked, the fruitlets slip off the central core, which remains on the bush. But when a blackberry is picked, core and all come off and we eat the whole thing.

Most blackberry bushes have extremely thorny stems, but the trailing variety has stems somewhat less threatening to berry pickers. This kind has been used in developing some of our popular modern berries—youngberries, loganberries (a cross between the raspberry and the blackberry), and boysenberries, which were developed from a chance blackberry seedling.

Probably our best-loved berries are strawberries, which are not true berries either. They too are aggregate fruits, each made up of many small, single-seed fruits around a

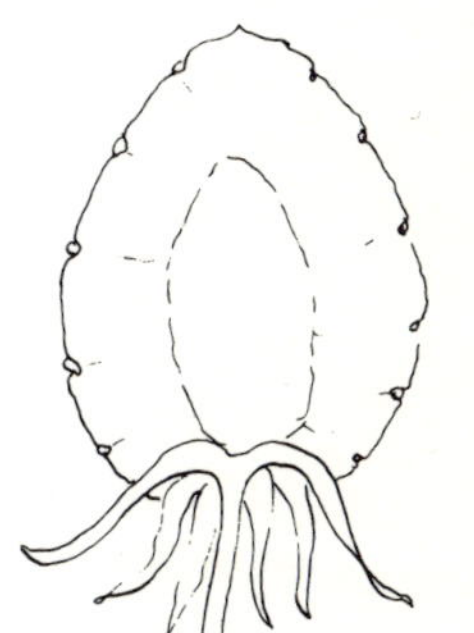

119

fleshy central core. The seeds are on the outside, embedded in the surface.

Since very early times, strawberries grew wild over most of Europe. By the fifteenth century, European gardeners were digging up wild plants and cultivating strawberries in their home gardens.

When the early settlers arrived here, they were delighted to find the delicious little fruits growing wild in the New World. A colonist in Maryland wrote home in a letter to his relatives in England, "Wee cannot sett downe a foote but tred on strawberries." The native American berries, though small, had a delicious flavor. Some of the American plants were taken to France, and from there to England and other European countries.

However, long before this time, the Indian people of Chile in South America had been cultivating a kind of strawberry plant that was better than any in Europe or North America. It was said that some of its fruits were as big as walnuts. When they were observed in 1782 by a French traveler, a Captain Frezier, he took some of the plants back with him to Europe.

Soon, Chilean and North American strawberry plants were growing side by side in European gardens. Before long, there was cross-pollination of the two kinds. Some of the hybrid seedlings that resulted bore many large, delicious fruits that combined the best qualities of the American and Chilean species. Some of them were brought over

120

to the United States, where they became the ancestors of the superior strawberry plants of today.

Strawberries are a popular fruit. We eat many of them fresh, as dessert fruits. Still more are used in strawberry jam, a special treat. This is usually made by boiling a fifty-fifty mixture of strawberries and sugar. But there is another, and older, way that you may want to try in summer when the days are hot and sunny.

SUNBERRY JAM

Clean and wash one pint of fresh ripe strawberries. Spread them on a towel to dry. Then slice the strawberries in half, lengthwise, into a shallow, flat-bottom pan. Add

121

two cupfuls of granulated sugar. Mix gently but thoroughly.

Wipe all traces of sugar and juice from the pan and cover it tightly with clear, transparent plastic wrap. Stand it outdoors in full sun. Bring it indoors at night.

In the morning, remove the plastic and stir the fruit. Then cover with a fresh sheet of plastic. Do this for at least four sunny days, until the mixture looks, smells, and tastes like strawberry jam. Spoon it into very clean jars and cover with plastic. Keep the jam in the refrigerator, and eat a little each day—on toast, pudding, or as a sauce for ice cream.

The strawberry plant is small and low and produces many runners. When a runner touches the soil, it takes root, producing a new plant. Not too many years ago, fresh strawberries were available only for a short time in summer, when all the berries ripened. Now, however, there are "ever-bearing" plants that have blossoms and fruits all through the year. These are easily grown by home gardeners, who plant them in small backyards, in flower-garden borders, and in pots and tubs. The leaves and runners are interesting, the flowers are attractive, and the fruits are delicious.

Index

The rich variety of fruits we find so readily available and so temptingly displayed in our modern supermarkets has become a commonplace to almost everybody. But the story of most of them began thousands of years ago as early man wandered from place to place, moving ever westward across the world. The apples, oranges and grapefruit, pineapples and peaches, dates, grapes and figs, and many of the other fruits we take so much for granted originally came from faraway lands and have their own special history, their own special place in nature's scheme of things. Young readers will find a wealth of fascinating information about these fruits in this lively book, informally written and charmingly illustrated with photographs and detailed drawings. The mysterious ways in which many are pollinated, how man has learned to cultivate and develop them to their present perfection by such means as cross-breeding and grafting, are explained in easy-to-understand fashion. The authors have included simple and delectable fruit recipes easily made at home and have given directions for such delightful home projects as planting an indoor grapefruit grove, raising an avocado tree indoors, and growing a pineapple plant of one's own.

ELIZABETH K. COOPER received her M.A. and Ph.D. degrees from the University of California at Los Angeles and has combined a notable teaching career with a highly successful one in writing books for children. *Sweet and Delicious* is Mrs. Cooper's third title for Golden Gate Junior Books. The others are *The Wild Cats Of Rome* and, co-authored by Padraic Cooper, *A Tree Is Something Wonderful*, published in 1972. Among her many titles for Harcourt Brace Jovanovich are, *And Everything Nice: The Story Of Sugar, Spices And Flavoring*, *Science In Your Own Backyard*, and *Science On The Shores And Banks*. Mrs. Cooper and her husband make their home in the Santa Monica Mountains overlooking the San Fernando Valley near Los Angeles.

PADRAIC COOPER, a free-lance photographer and horticulturalist, was born and grew up in Santa Monica, California. He obtained his B.A. in fine arts from Chouinard Art Institute and did graduate work in photography at San Fernando Valley State College. A number of Mr. Cooper's photographs have appeared in elementary science texts published by Harcourt Brace Jovanovich. In addition, he cultivates rare and exotic plants and manages his own plant shop in Southern California.